MW01290920

1

HOCKEY'S ROYAL FAMILY

THE CONACHERS

"stuff of legends"

PAUL WHITE

Copyright © 2015 by Paul White

All rights reserved. No part of this book may be reproduced or transmitted in any form or by any means, electronic or mechanical, including photocopying, or by any information storage or retrieval system, without permission in writing from the publisher (who is the author Paul White).

ISBN: 9781517460877

Contents

Foreword

Who is hockey's royal family?

There are many great hockey players to consider. Hockey families that need consideration include: Gordie Howe and his sons Mark Howe and Marty Howe; Montreal Canadiens' legends Maurice "Rocket" Richard and his brother Henri Richard; Chicago Black Hawks stars Bobby Hull and his brother Dennis, and Bobby's son Brett Hull; Frank Mahovlich and his brother Peter Mahovlich also warrant consideration. Modern era families such as Eric Staal and his brothers Marc, Jordan and Jared must receive some consideration. There are many others including the Patricks, the Sutters who could all be added to the list of contenders for the title of hockey's royal family.

When one takes the time to consider the number of families who have sent more than one member to the NHL, the impact of these brothers, or fathers and sons, has been significant upon the history of this great game. But there is one family whose contributions to the great game of ice hockey stands above even this list of great hockey families.

However, there can only be one Royal Family of Hockey, the Conachers.

First of all, Lionel, Charlie and Roy are the only three brothers to be inducted as Honoured Members in the Hockey Hall of Fame. The list of scoring titles, all-star game appearances, Stanley Cup and league championships, not to mention other unique hockey achievements are well-documented in this hockey history book. Toronto Maple Leaf fans will be interested to know that Charlie Conacher scored game-winning goals in the first Stanley Cup Championship won by the Maple Leafs and his nephew Brian Conacher scored game-winning goals in the last Stanley Cup to be won by a Toronto hockey team. All three brothers were multi-sport stars who are honoured members of several sports halls of fame. Lionel Conacher's multi-sport achievements were recognized in 1950 when he was named Canada's Athlete of the First Half Century. The Conachers were not just goal scorers, Lionel and his nephew Murray Henderson were defensemen; Roy and his nephew Pete were smooth-skating forwards who finessed their way to the net; Charlie was a power forward who led the league in scoring primarily because of his booming shot; and Brian was primarily a defensive-minded forward with a knack for scoring key goals. As the pages of this book illustrate, the exploits of Lionel, Charlie, Roy and Bert as well as their sons Pete and Brian and their nephew Murray Henderson, there never has been a family who dominated the history of this great game like the Conachers!

Introduction

The achievements of the Conacher family is the "stuff of legends". The oldest, Lionel, would set the standard that would challenge not only his younger siblings, but would be the watermark for athletes in a wide variety of sports. He starred in many sports, winning championships as both an amateur and a professional. Adding to the lustre of his mystique as a sports legend, Lionel, on at least two occasions, played on two teams in two different sports on the same day, capturing two championship titles on each of those occasions. When he finally hung up his skates, boxing gloves, lacrosse stick, football helmet, and baseball cleats, he was inducted into several sports halls of fame.

Lionel was more than an individualist, he was the consummate team player with great leadership capabilities. During his athletic career Lionel was a member of two Stanley Cup champion teams; one Memorial Cup champion hockey team; one Grey Cup winning football club; countless other title winning teams; and he won the Canadian light-heavyweight boxing crown and various other boxing and wrestling titles. He was also member of several NHL All-Star teams.

When he completed his athletic career, Lionel used his sporting fame, in part, to create a new legacy for himself and his family. He became a successful entrepreneur and politician, serving in both the Ontario Legislature and the Canadian Parliament.

Not to be outdone, younger brother Charlie, carved a formidable sporting legend for himself. He enjoyed a Hall of Fame hockey career, winning the Memorial Cup and the Stanley Cup, as well as earning league scoring titles and being selected to various All-Star teams. And, like Lionel, he too realized success in the business world. Ironically, after being raised in near-poverty conditions, Charlie's life after hockey included business associations with oil and gas magnates like Max Bell and Frank McMahon, not to mention Hollywood star Bing Crosby!

Their children would follow in their fathers' footsteps achieving success in the world of sports and business. Both Charlie's son, Pete, and Lionel's son, Brian, would achieve positions in the world of hockey as members of NHL teams. Two of Lionel's other sons, Lionel Jr. and David, would gain recognition in the sport of football.

The Conacher sports legend began with their parents, Benjamin and Elizabeth Conacher, who raised 10 children, 5 girls and 5 boys, on a meagre income of $20 a week. Their offspring would create athletic exploits that were the talk of their hometown, Toronto, and for some, the legend would span the country and the continent! For many of them there was a realization that accomplishments in the world of sports could translate into success for their economic and social ambitions.

In fact, they would come to be known in many circles as hockey's royal family!

Mark Conacher, the son of Hockey Hall of Fame legend Roy Conacher, told a reporter, "I feel the story of the Conachers illustrates what sport can do, it was what made poverty bearable for them."[1]

Most everyone knows about the athletic accomplishments of the Conacher boys, Lionel, Charlie, Roy and Bert, but according to Mark Conacher, their sisters "were the best, but the opportunities didn't exist"[2] for women compared to the opportunities that were available to male athletes.

What is of particular significance is the fact that the Conacher brothers, Lionel and Charlie, were enjoying amazing successes in the world of sports and beginning to build much of the wealth that would bode well for the rest of their lives, and that of their children. And all of this was achieved during the middle of the Great Depression!

This is further evidence of the drive and determination of the boys from Scollard Street to climb out of poverty and enjoy a life of wealth and economic power for themselves and their families!

In 1998, Jim Proudfoot, the Hall of Fame sports writer for the **Toronto Star** wrote, "Here is the great Toronto book nobody has written." In the pages that follow you will discover that Mr. Proudfoot's wish has been answered!

Chapter One

<u>The Conacher Family</u>

Benjamin[3] and Elizabeth[4] Conacher raised ten children, five girls and five boys[5]. Benjamin supported his family as a teamster, driving his horse and wagon around Toronto working at odd jobs. Probably because of the tenuous family income, the Conacher family moved several times to various rental accommodations[6] until they finally settled at 122 Scollard Street in the Yorkville area of North Toronto.

On May 24, 1901, Benjamin and Elizabeth welcomed a son, Lionel Joseph Pretoria Conacher, into their family, a little brother for their daughter Dolly.

It was a different world in Toronto at that time compared to today. Although settlers - mostly of British and Irish origin - had lived in what was at first called York, for more than a century, Canada had yet to celebrate its fortieth birthday when the Conacher's first son was born. The ties to Britain were still evident. In fact, one of Lionel's middle names was "Pretoria". The origin of this middle name is unknown, but it was probably due to the fact that at that time Britain and its Empire were embroiled in the Boer War in South Africa and Pretoria was the name of one of the principal towns in that country.

Fifty years later, this baby boy would be acclaimed as Canada's Athlete of the Half Century.

Lionel and his nine siblings attended Jesse Ketchum Public School. It was here that the Conacher kids participated in what would today be called "social networking". Without the technological innovations of the modern era it was the playground of their school yard where most of the social interactions occurred.

The Jesse Ketchum playground provided the venue where the Conacher boys and girls and their school chums were not only introduced to a wide range of sports, but they were encouraged to hone their skills in these activities. This promotion of athleticism was encouraged by the school principal William Kirk, not just because he was an avid sports enthusiast, but because he felt that if the students "participated in games, they'd learn to love them and they'd stay out of trouble"[7].

This environment not only encouraged sporting skills but also may have been at the root of the idea of using sports as a vehicle to elevate their lifestyle upwards and away from the poverty of their youth.

After all, it was not just a few of the Conachers who became interested in sports. Lionel's, Charlie's, and Roy's athletic endeavours are well known and well documented, but they were not the only top-flight athletes in the family. Roy's twin brother Bert was an exceptional hockey player, but an eye injury suffered in a game of road hockey at the age of 16 curtailed any chances for him to have a future in the NHL. Some experts suggest that Bert might have been the best of them all! Twin sisters, Nora and Kay were star athletes in their own right. Each of the girls earned accolades in baseball as well as track and field events.

On February 12, 1902, Lionel's first, baby brother, Dermot was born. It was said that "Dermot was a pretty good footballer" but some war experiences really shook him up and that was the end of his athletic endeavours.[8] There is not much known of Dermot's life. The **Toronto Daily Sta**r reported in its "Obituaries" in the April 21, 1969 edition, that Dermot B. Conacher had passed away leaving his wife Helen and two sons, Don and Hugh.

Chapter Two

Lionel Conacher

Lionel Joseph Pretoria "The Big Train" Conacher was born May 24, 1901, the second oldest of the Conacher children.

The Conacher family were very poor when Lionel and his siblings were growing up. His father, Ben, worked hard to provide the necessities of life for his family working as a teamster.

Seeing his father work hard to support his family, and yet their living conditions always seemed too meagre, must have been a great motivating force for Lionel. This might in fact have provided great incentive for many of the decisions that he would make throughout his life.

Lionel always excelled at sports. Although he dropped out of school after Grade Eight, it should not be construed that he was not intelligent. Actually, the opposite was closer to the truth. He quickly learned that making the most of his physical attributes and athletic abilities could be his ticket to a better life. Ironically, it was his father who had perhaps planted this seed in his mind. Lionel once told a reporter about a lesson that he learned from his father saying, "Dad always drilled home to me that brawn is useless in sport unless brains are combined with it".[9] And his successes, both on and off the field of sports, definitely illustrate that Lionel paid heed to his father's words.

In the future, as Lionel experienced success in the world of sports, he, in turn, would prove to be a compelling force in the lives of his siblings, especially Charlie, encouraging them to seek a life in sports, not only because of the immediate rewards, but as a means of escaping the poverty of their childhood.

Many consider Lionel to be the greatest athlete in Canadian sports history. Conacher was not a one-sport athlete. Nor did he merely "dabble" in a number of sports. No, Lionel Conacher was a recognized star in several sports. His athletic achievements resulted in his being inducted into the halls of fame of several sports. In recognition of his wide-ranging athletic abilities, in 1950 Lionel Conacher was named Canada's Athlete of the First Half Century.

In a eulogy of sorts, after Lionel's untimely death in 1954, the **Toronto Daily Star** described the broad range of his athletic talents as they related to the sports and lesser-known athletic events that he participated in:

> Lionel Conacher's stamina and proficiency in many athletic sports made him a miracle man. He excelled in football, hockey, baseball and lacrosse. He won the light-heavyweight boxing championship of Canada in 1920 and sparred four rounds with Jack Dempsey in 1922 in an exhibition at

Christie Street hospital. He was a strong sculler and swimmer, ran 100 yards in less than 11 seconds in a baseball uniform, and was better than good at soccer.[10]

It is fitting that a Canadian sporting legend would begin his journey to the stature of Canadian sporting icon by playing ice hockey!

However, before Conacher could play organized hockey he had to learn to skate. Surprisingly, despite the fact that his friends and siblings had learned to skate while attending Jesse Ketchum School, for some reason, Lionel had never learned this skill!

Today, hockey "experts" claim that if a youngster does not learn how to skate and begin playing hockey at a very early age, they will never have the time, or the opportunity, to develop the skills necessary to play competitive hockey, let alone star in the National Hockey League. If that thought process was passed on to Lionel, he either ignored it, or used it as a motivation to prove them wrong. After all, Conacher was well into his teen years before he even learned how to skate.

An example of his determination to develop hockey skills can be seen in a comment that Lionel once made when he described what he endured as he worked to hone his skating skills. "The average kid starts skating at the age of seven years or younger. I laced on skates for the first time at the age of sixteen, and you'll never know the humiliation and utter dreariness of the long hours which I spent on rinks with younger and much more skilled players before I won a post in junior circles".[11]

His hard work and determination to overcome the odds found almost immediate success. Within a year of beginning to learn to skate, Lionel tried out for, and made the Toronto Aura Lee junior hockey team. He skated with that club for both the 1917-18 and 1918-19 hockey seasons.

After just three years of learning to skate and developing hockey skills and experience, which included only two years of playing in an organized hockey league, Conacher was asked to join the Toronto Canoe Club Paddlers. This uniquely named junior hockey team was a powerhouse in Ontario Hockey Association junior ranks at that time. There were rumblings that the team that was assembled for the 1919-20 hockey season was essentially an all-star team of players plucked from other organizations. Lionel's invitation to join this team speaks volumes about not only his natural athletic talents, but his determination and dedication to improving himself as a hockey player.

It was during his season with the Canoe Club Paddlers that Lionel earned the first[12] of many of the sporting championships and honours that he would receive in his athletic career. His team captured the Canadian Junior Hockey Championship, the Memorial Cup. And Lionel's contribution was quite significant. During his team's 13-game stretch to the Memorial Cup, Conacher notched 23 goals and 10 assists.[13] His scoring statistics were exceptional for this era of hockey, which was a notoriously low-scoring period of time in the sport. Whereas one might be forgiven for thinking that Lionel was a high-scoring forward when in fact he was a defenceman!

Three years later, in the spring of 1923, Conacher would return to the Memorial Cup championship. This time not as a player, but as a referee! The two-game playoff for the right to claim supremacy in Canadian junior hockey was held in Kitchener, Ontario. His skating skills and hockey knowledge had progressed to the point where Conacher was given the job of officiating both games between the western champions from the University of Manitoba, and the host eastern champions, the Kitchener Colts.

It has often been said that football was Lionel's favourite sport and that his athletic talents were most suited to the gridiron. Conacher first stepped on to the football field at the age of eleven and it was not long before he tasted success in that sport. From 1912 through to 1915, his team, the Toronto Capitals, captured the Toronto city league championship every year. But that was not the end of his youthful football experiences and successes. In 1918, Lionel led the Toronto Central YMCA junior football team to the Ontario Championship. The next football season, he joined the intermediate football club, which made it to the provincial finals, only to lose to the "gridders" from Sarnia.

By 1920, Conacher had moved to the Toronto Rugby Club of

the senior football loop. Once again he found himself on a championship team, capturing the Ontario Rugby Football Union title. But, in the Interprovincial play downs, they lost to the Toronto Argonauts.

Despite his team's defeat, the Argos were so impressed by Lionel's play that they invited him to suit up with them for the 1921 football season. As an Argonaut, Lionel did not disappoint himself, his team, or the fans. The Argonauts won all of their six games to lead the league in the 1921 football season. Conacher led the league in scoring with 14 touchdowns and 85 points.

As the high-flying Argos prepared for the championship game they were about to enter into previously uncharted territory in terms of contending for the Canadian football title. The 1921 final contest featured the first-ever Grey Cup game between teams representing both eastern and western Canada. Lionel and his teammates continued their dominance in Canadian football. The Argonauts captured the coveted trophy by trampling their western foes, the Edmonton Eskimos, by a 23-0 score.

On that Grey Cup day, Lionel Conacher etched another unbelievable feat into an already growing legend of athletic prowess. With the Argos leading the Eskimos 23-0, Lionel left the game at the end of the third quarter, in order to switch uniforms and sports. After a quick trip across Toronto he joined his Toronto Aura Lee senior hockey club in time to help them defeat the Toronto Granites and capture the Sportsman's Athletic Association Trophy. Two championships in one day, not a bad outing for Lionel Conacher!

The next football season, Lionel earned the moniker that would follow him for the rest of his life. Even today, more than sixty years after his death, he is still known as, "The Big Train". That 1922 season, his dominance on the football field was total! Like a "Big Train" he steamed over his opposition, leading the league in rushing, carrying the ball for an incredible 950 yards in only 6 games.

After Conacher's Argonauts had practically clinched the Big Four football title in 1922, Lionel's supremacy as talented football player was best described by Doug Chilman, the secretary of the rival Hamilton Tigers, who told a Toronto reporter, "Chain Conacher up and we can make your team of champions look like the tail-enders of the sand lot league."[14]

Commenting upon Conacher's prowess on the football field, legendary sports writer, Lou Marsh, described Lionel as "the superman of Canadian football", and as to his performance in the game Marsh wrote that Lionel "stood out like a red vest at a funeral."[15]

The next football season, 1923, Lionel would be the centre of controversy in the championship game of Ontario Rugby Football Union between the footballers from Toronto and Hamilton. With the score tied, Toronto sent Conacher on to the field. Lionel's appearance, caused the Hamilton team to pull their players from the field. At that time, league rules required that players must have residency in the community where they played. Hamilton contended that Conacher lived in Pennsylvania[16] and therefore, was ineligible to play for the Toronto club. The O.R.F.U. agreed, and the Tigers were awarded the league's title.[17]

Two years later, in 1925, Lionel was once again at the centre of another Canadian football controversy. This time, it was the Montreal football club that challenged Conacher's right to play for Toronto. It was Montreal's contention that Lionel was being paid to play hockey in Pennsylvania and therefore was a professional hockey player. As the Montreal players were amateurs, there was a fear that they would lose that status if they were to engage Lionel on the field of play.[18] One has to wonder if much of the contention around Conacher playing for Toronto was based more on a dread of facing his great football talents, than on a question of amateur vs. professional status.

In 1922, Lionel played for another championship team. However, this time he would claim top honours in yet another sport, lacrosse. He starred for the Toronto Maitlands whom he led to the Ontario Lacrosse title.

Two years later, on June 9, 1924, Conacher was once again instrumental in the Maitlands' successful journey to lacrosse supremacy in the Province of Ontario. That day provided another remarkable page in the saga that would become Lionel Conacher's epic sports career. What happened that day is just another indicator of the amazing sporting skills that Lionel Conacher possessed.

The day began with Conacher playing baseball for the Toronto Hillcrests in the championship game. When Lionel came to bat in the bottom of the ninth inning, his team was trailing by one run. The bases were loaded and Conacher smacked a double to centre field, scoring the tying and winning runs to capture not only the game, but the league title as well! Lionel quickly left the baseball park and headed across town to Scarborough Beach to join his Toronto Maitlands lacrosse team which was embroiled in the final game of the Ontario Amateur Lacrosse title match.

The lacrosse game was at half time when Lionel arrived. The Maitlands were trailing Brampton Excelsiors by a 2-1 score. However, by the time the final buzzer sounded, Conacher had once again worked his athletic magic. He netted two goals, while helping to hold the Brampton squad off the score sheet. The Maitlands captured the Ontario Championship with a 3-2 victory. Lionel Conacher had his second championship in one day. Not a bad day for any athlete![19]

In 1951 Lionel Conacher was inducted as a Charter Member into Canada's Lacrosse Hall of Fame.

After the Toronto Canoe Club Paddlers had successfully captured the Memorial Cup and his junior hockey career ended,

Lionel moved on to the Ontario Hockey Association's senior loop, suiting up with Toronto Aura Lee's senior club. After winning the Memorial Cup, Lionel had become the target of professional hockey teams who wished him to forsake the amateur ranks and play hockey for money.

It was reported in local newspapers that the Montreal Canadiens were about to make a contract offer to Lionel. However, despite the offer of a lucrative hockey contract, Conacher's goals for his future went further than simply getting a professional sports contract. The Christmas Day edition of the Toronto **Globe and Mail** provides a telling description of the hockey player's plans.

> By sheer determination, cleverness, grit and ability to assimilate punishment Conacher has developed from a mediocre player into one of the stars of the O.H.A. He has set out a course to follow and has not deviated from it. He was a junior for two years believes that he will improve more rapidly by playing at least one more year in the O.H.A. senior series.[20]

The same newspaper story revealed that the Canadiens were not the only team interested in Lionel's services saying that he had "received tempting offers from other clubs, but his answer has always been in the negative"[21].

A look into the future would reveal that Lionel was establishing a template that his children, especially his youngest son,

Brian, would follow as they considered their options between professional sports and other areas of endeavours, including furthering their education.

One of those tempting offers, which he spurned, had come from the Toronto St. Pats. His hometown team had offered him a $3,000 contract with a $500 signing bonus to play the 1920-21 NHL hockey season.[22]

This was a lucrative offer for a professional hockey contract at that time. For instance, in 1924, Eddie Shore, who would arguably become one of the greatest defencemen in the history of the NHL, signed a contract to play with Regina of the Western Hockey league for only $1,000.[23]

By this time, Lionel had filled out physically to a muscular 200 pounds on a six-foot frame. His physical attributes combined with his tremendous skills made him a popular target for teams representing a variety of sports.

The only drawback to these professional contract offers was Lionel's true love, the sport of football. He had enjoyed much success playing for the Toronto Argonauts. If he signed a contract to play professional hockey he would be ineligible to play football, which was still an amateur sport. To help him justify turning down a professional hockey contract, Harris Ardiel, a family friend, helped Lionel land a job working for a bank. The income earned from this employment would allow him to pursue other amateur sports.

Ignoring overtures from professional hockey teams in order to remain an amateur athlete sounds very nice, but one has to wonder if Lionel's decision may have been for other reasons. It seems he was looking to create opportunities that would have a long term benefit. This meant improving his education. In the next couple of years he would make a dramatic decision that would surprise many of his fans.

At the same time another professional sport came calling for Lionel's services. It was reported that Ed Holly, a former member of the Toronto Maple Leafs baseball team, who was a scout for the Boston Red Sox, had sent Conacher a letter offering him a contract to play professional baseball. Conacher's response to this overture was reported in the newspaper. "Conacher says that he has no intention of playing professional baseball or of playing any other game as a professional. He says that he intends to stay in the amateur ranks."[24]

To add to the allure of what was becoming an overwhelming display of Lionel's athletic abilities, at the same time as he was receiving contract offers, Lionel boxed his way to the Canadian Amateur Light Heavyweight boxing title. All of this was happening and Conacher was still only 20 years old!

In 1922 Eddie Livingstone, the former owner of a Toronto professional hockey franchise claimed that Conacher was being paid "under the table" to maintain his amateur status. An irate Conacher sued for libel. When Lionel won his suit, Livingstone did not have to pay money to Conacher. Instead, Livingstone was ordered to issue apologies in various newspapers.

Lionel suited up to play intermediate hockey for North Toronto for the 1922-23 hockey season. Once again Conacher's scoring prowess was evident. In a six-game playoff run he notched 12 goals and four assists.

During that hockey campaign Conacher would play a dramatic role in another historic moment in the sport of hockey. On February 8, 1923, Norman Albert, a sports reporter for the **Toronto Daily Star**, broadcast the third period of a playoff game between North Toronto and Midland at the Toronto Arena Gardens. This was the first time that any part of a hockey game had ever been broadcast on a radio station. Radio station CFRA was owned by the **Toronto Daily Star**. On this historic occasion, Lionel scored 6 goals to lead his team to victory.[25]

NOTE: Historic moments seem to have followed Lionel throughout his career, and his life, for that matter. Not only did he play in the first hockey game to be broadcast on radio, but he also played in the first hockey game to be aired on television. It happened in Bracebridge, Ontario on January 25, 1952 featuring two teams of NHL Oldtimers. The game was taped by the American television network, NBC for rebroadcast. All four of the hockey-playing

Conacher brothers took part in this significant event accounting "for five of the 13 goals scored. As well as Bert's three, Charlie potted 2, Lionel drew an assist on the picture play of the game".[26]

In a non-sporting event, perhaps hoping to cash in on his rising sports celebrity in Toronto in 1922, Lionel opened what would become the first of many entrepreneurial ventures, "Burch and Conacher's Men's Clothes Shop". His partner was Billy Burch who, along with Lionel, had been a member of the Toronto Canoe Club Memorial Cup Champion team in 1920. The two would later be teammates with the New York Americans in the NHL.[27]

The shop was located at 233 Yonge Street and advertised that it carried "a complete line of more conservative styles".[28]

Conacher seemed to be constantly aware of the need to improve himself and his opportunities. He was determined to advance his economic status for himself and his family. To further that goal he registered at the Bellefonte Academy in Pennsylvania with an eye on attaining an academic standing that would allow him to seek a university education. After a year at this prep school, he was one step closer to achieving his goal. Lionel's next step would be to enrol at nearby Duquesne University in Pittsburgh, Pennsylvania.

Before leaving for Pennsylvania, Conacher made another large change in his personal life. On September 17, 1923 Lionel married Dorothy Kennedy. They would have five children,

Constance, Diane, Lionel Jr., David, and Brian.

It was not just a "books and study" situation only, while he attended Bellefonte Academy, or later when he was studying at Duquesne University, Lionel also continued to enjoy playing football, suiting up for the school team. He also played hockey, skating with the Pittsburgh Yellowjackets of the USAHA-West regional division.

The Yellowjackets, with Lionel leading the playoffs in scoring with 5 goals in 8 games, captured the regional title in the 1923-24 hockey season and then went on to capture the United States Amateur Hockey championship.

The argument could be made that the Yellowjackets benefited from Conacher's presence on the team for reasons other than his skills as a hockey player. He helped his team by encouraging a couple of his friends, both future Hockey Hall of Famers, centreman Harold "Baldy" Cotton and goalie Roy "Shrimp" Worters, to move to Pittsburgh and play on the team.

Lionel's Yellowjackets repeated their successes with another U.S. Amateur hockey title in the 1924-25 season. Interestingly, many of the players skating with the Pittsburgh club were Canadian.[29] It is known that Conacher had convinced Cotton and Worters to move to Pennsylvania, but one has to wonder how many of the others were playing for the Yellowjackets because of Lionel's influence.

The 1924-25 hockey campaign would be Lionel's last as an amateur hockey player. The next season, he signed to play with the Pittsburgh Pirates, who were first-year members of the National Hockey League. Conacher's contract to leave the amateur ranks of sports was a record at that time - a three-year deal for $7,500 per season.[30]

On November 26, 1925, Lionel etched his name in the NHL's history book by scoring the Pirates' first-ever goal as Pittsburgh defeated Boston to claim their first NHL victory in their first game.

In their first season, the expansion Pirates experienced some success as they finished 3rd in the regular season standings and made the playoffs. Once again Lionel's prowess as an offensive defenceman was evident. He notched 9 goals and 4 assists in 33 regular season games. Unfortunately, Pittsburgh's "Cinderella season" came to an abrupt end when they were eliminated from post-season play by the Montreal Maroons in just two games.

After he signed a contract to play professional hockey with Pittsburgh in the NHL, Lionel was free to pursue other professional sporting opportunities. In January of 1926 he inked a deal to play professional baseball with the Toronto Maple Leafs. That season Conacher added another championship to his growing list of sports accomplishments when the Maple Leafs captured the 1926 Triple "A" baseball crown.[31]

Conacher's baseball talents may not have been up to his usual skill levels compared to the other sports that he played, especially when you consider the comments about his abilities on the baseball diamond made by his Triple "A" manager Dan Howley who said, "When he's in right field, he ought to wear a mask, but I'll say this – he can hit some!"[32]

Lionel's time as a hockey player in Pittsburgh came to a sudden end during the early part of the 1926-27 hockey season. After only nine games, he was dealt to the New York Americans for Charlie Langlois and $2,000 cash. Conacher made an impact in his first season in New York recording 8 goals and 9 assists from his defensive position. His 17 scoring points were the second best on the team. However, the Americans finished out of the playoffs.

The 1927-28 season spelled the same lack of success for New York as once again they missed post-season play. Lionel continued to demonstrate his offensive prowess on the ice, netting 11 goals and 6 assists. Once again his point total was second best on the team.

The following season, Lionel became more like a lion in his style of play receiving a whopping 132 penalty minutes in 1928-29 which led the team in that statistical category, and not surprisingly, his point production dropped dramatically to 5 goals and 2 assists.

Conacher assumed the dual duties of player/coach of the Americans for the 1929-30 hockey season. Despite his added responsibility to guide the team as its coach, Lionel still led the club in penalties. This time with a more moderate 73 minutes. His point production increased to four goals and six assists. Notwithstanding his promotion to the position of coach, it was evident that something was wrong with Lionel's game.

As the 1930-31 season was about to begin, the Americans traded their coach and defenceman to the Montreal Maroons. The Americans could not even garner another player from Montreal in the transaction. Instead, they received an undisclosed amount of cash.

His trade to the Maroons may have been one of the lowest points of Lionel Conacher's sporting career. It seems that Lionel had worn out his welcome in the "Big Apple". It was well-known around the league at that time that the Americans were a hard-partying lot and it was common knowledge that Lionel was an eager participant in the celebrating that occurred before and after every game.

His arrival in Montreal did not improve his hockey production, or his lifestyle. At one point in the season, the Maroons put him on waivers and not one team in the entire NHL was interested in taking Conacher!

In the off-season, Lionel realized that he needed to straighten out his life in order to continue playing hockey and earning a living to support his family. After all, his family was undergoing an expansion of sorts. On November 25, 1930 his family had increased in number with the birth of his first child, Constance.

The arrival of his baby daughter must have been a huge motivator for Lionel. Conacher promised his wife that the partying lifestyle was over and things would be different. Then he set about to do exactly that. He described how he was able to change the habits that had driven his lifestyle into such a downward spiral:

> It was in 1930 that I experienced my hardest battle as an athlete. At that time I had been in the National Hockey League for four years, only to find myself an unwanted veteran with the Montreal Maroons who were trying, unsuccessfully, to waive me out of the league. I promptly decided to quit drinking, and it was the training of many gruelling years in sports, making the old willpower say 'Uncle', that stood me in good stead. I've never touched a drink from that day…" [33]

Veteran journalist, Andy O'Brien described how Conacher went about changing his habits, recalling, "I used to watch him (Lionel) drink nine Cokes and eat a box of chocolates before going to bed, but he licked the craving…"[34]

Evidence of Lionel's lifestyle and the impact of his use of alcohol on his actions at this time appears evident from a Toronto court report published in the June 29, 1927:

> W.R. Miller testified that when he was a spectator at a ball game at Willowdale Park, Lionel Conacher, well-known athlete, bounded through the crowd and grasped him, broke his nose, blackened his eyes and lacerated his face. Miller stated that Conacher was under the influence of liquor and had attempted to strike his, Miller's father, but he intervened with result that he himself was beaten up. Magistrate Jones without hearing further evidence, committed Conacher for trial.[35]

In the summer of 1930 Lionel added another job in the wide world of sports to his resume. He became a lacrosse referee. Commenting upon Conacher's appointment by the Ontario Lacrosse Association, the **Toronto Daily Star** was effusive in its description of the impact the Association's newest referee had on the sport:

> It is very seldom that a referee occupies any of the spotlight, but with Conacher holding forth in his new role such will be the case. The big fellow has the reputation of being a qualified success at anything he has ever tackled in the line of sport, and his new interest is apparently no exception. He has developed into one of the few referees who is popular with all players and club officials alike.[36]

Playing hockey in Montreal afforded Lionel another opportunity to earn money as a professional athlete while playing in a sport other than hockey. In 1931, the Maroons were awarded a franchise in the newly-formed International Indoor Professional Lacrosse League.

The new league featured four teams, the Toronto Maple Leafs, the Montreal Canadiens, the Cornwall Colts and the Montreal Maroons. Lionel led the Maroons to the league championship and captured the scoring title with 107 points. His dominance as a lacrosse player was amply evident in the league scoring statistics where he outpaced his closest competitor by more than 50 scoring points![37]

It was in this new league's inaugural season that Conacher was honoured by his hometown. In his newspaper column, **Toronto Daily Star** sports editor W.A. Hewitt wrote that there were plans to hold a "Lionel Conacher Night" at an upcoming game between the Toronto Maple Leafs and Montreal Maroons lacrosse teams.

Hewitt was effusive in his rationale for such an honour being extended to Lionel, writing:

> Conacher has come back to his own home town many times before in uniforms of various teams and it is felt by the men behind the Conacher Night that it is time Toronto paid some special tribute to this giant, who ranks as the best all-round athlete ever developed in this sport-loving town.[38]

The next season, the lacrosse league folded, but Conacher found another professional sport to occupy his summer season. He signed a contract to wrestle professionally! This would not be his first exposure to the wrestling ring. At the age of 16, he had captured the Ontario Amateur Wrestling crown fighting in the 125 pound weight class. He had also developed a reputation as a good boxer and probably the highlight of his boxing career had been a four-round exhibition match with the legendary Jack Dempsey.

It was announced that his first professional wrestling match would be against Carl Pospeshil on May 3, 1932 and it would be broadcast on radio station CFRA.

Lionel won all 26 matches[39] that he wrestled that summer before returning to Montreal for the upcoming NHL hockey season.

An interesting comment in the **Montreal Herald** that was re-printed in the **Toronto Daily Star** suggests that Lionel may not have been all that interested in remembering his professional wrestling career.

> According to the **Montreal Herald**, Lionel Conacher smacked Nels Stewart down in Boston because Stewart had referred to Conacher as "Connie the Clutch". The **Toronto Star** wrote that "Mr. Conacher has no wish to be reminded of his professional wrestling days and what he did to Stewart is a tip-off on how he feels about being so maligned.[40]

In 1933, Conacher was instrumental in helping create a professional football league. The new gridiron group featured teams from Toronto and Montreal as well as two New York State entries from Rochester and Buffalo. Although he had not played football for many years, Lionel announced that he would suit up as the captain of the Toronto Crosse and Blackwell Chefs.

When it was originally publicized that Lionel was at the forefront of the creation of this new football league, the **Toronto Daily Star** went to great lengths to describe how, and why, the league, especially the Toronto team, would find success:

> Canada's greatest all-round athlete is confident that the league will go over with a bang if given the proper chance. Ten thousand people paid to see the famous Red Grange when he paid a flying visit to Toronto with two professional teams from the south (the United States) several years ago and there is no reason why Conacher, Red Moore and Yip Foster should not be able to fill the place.[41]

The article went on to say that Lionel planned on bringing to the team several hockey players who had lost their amateur status when they signed professional hockey contracts. Although it had been several years since "Harold Cotton, Duke McCurry, Jess Spring, Fred Ogden, and Chucker Cliff" and several others had played football, they were all eager to play again. And, there is probably little doubt that the league hoped to cash in on the presence of several hockey stars.[42]

Although Lionel had been away from football for many years, it was evident that he still possessed the skills necessary to dominate. In a report of a game played in Rochester, the article was effusive in its description of Conacher's domination of the game in spite of the fact that his team had lost 12-6. The report from Rochester said, "Lionel Conacher was the whole show" and it went on to say,

> The great kicking of Lionel Conacher perhaps saved the invaders from a more one-sided defeat. Never before has there been such an exhibition of punting seen in the stadium as this great Canadian star exhibited last night. Towering boots of 60 to 65 yards were common, and it was his educated toe that paved the way for the lone Toronto touchdown.[43]

The same newspaper report stated that as well as his punting contributions, Lionel accounted for "90 per cent of the ground-gaining" for the Toronto football club.[44]

Lionel continued playing professional football into the 1934 season. At that time, his Toronto team had garnered new sponsors and a new moniker, the Toronto Wrigley Aromints.[45]

With the return of the NHL season in the autumn of 1933, Lionel found himself on the move. On October 1, 1933 the Maroons traded to him to Chicago for Teddy Graham. This would turn out to be only a one-year hiatus in Chicago. But it would prove to be a fortunate turn of events for Conacher. He recorded 10 goals and 13 assists, his best goal production in several seasons, and he anchored the Black Hawks defence to capture his, and the Black Hawks, first Stanley Cup Championship.

LIONEL CONACHER —CHICAGO BLACKHAWKS
Defense   Career Record—Goals 80
            Assists 105, Points 185
        Born Toronto, Ont. May 24, 1900
No. 12   1964-65 CANADIAN/AMERICAN GREATS

On February 14, 1934, Lionel suited up with a team of NHL All-Stars to face his brother Charlie and his Toronto Maple Leafs in the first-ever NHL All-Star game. The match was played to benefit Toronto Maple Leaf star "Ace" Bailey who had been injured in a serious on-ice incident in a hockey game in Boston. Bailey's hockey career had come to a sudden end due to an injury incurred by a vicious attack on him by Bruins star Eddie Shore.

His stay in the "Windy City" lasted only one season. About one year from the time of his arrival in Chicago on October 3, 1934, Lionel found himself on his way back to Montreal. This time, however, he was headed to the Montreal Canadiens. The deal involved six players, Conacher, Leroy Goldsworthy and Roger Jenkins to Montreal for Lorne Chabot, Marty Burke and former Montreal superstar Howie Morenz who were headed to Chicago.

But before the ink had dried on that deal, the Habs dispensed Conacher to their cross-town rivals, and his former team, the Montreal Maroons. That October 3rd deal sent Lionel and Herb Cain to the Maroons in exchange for Nels Crutchfield.

Lionel's return to the Maroons proved to be as eventful as his previous season in Chicago. First, he anchored the defence corps as the Maroons captured what would be that franchise's last Stanley Cup Championship. And, he was named to the NHL's First All-Star Team. This was an improvement over his Second All-Star Team placement the previous hockey season.

In 1935, no doubt hoping to take advantage of their fame in the world of sports, especially as NHL hockey stars, in a totally non-athletic endeavour, Lionel and his brother Charlie, opened a gas service station. Located at Yonge Street and Davenport Road, not too far from their childhood home, this venture was an immediate success as sports fans lined up to fill their automobile gas tanks, hoping to catch a glimpse of one, or both, of the station's famous owners.

Conacher was a rock-solid "defensive-defenceman" who logged a 12-year career in the NHL. Lionel was often near the top of the league in penalty minutes, but he also scored many goals, which

44

was remarkable considering that he played in an era that was noted for low-scoring and many forwards did not accumulate a significant number of scoring points each season.

In November 1936, a group of players from the New York Americans were sitting in the stands at Maple Leaf Gardens on a practice day discussing a story that was circulating that Lionel was considering retirement despite the fact that he was having a tremendous season. Conacher's Maroons were coming to Toronto to play the Leafs. A sports reporter asked the players from the New York club how you could effectively stop Lionel from leading the attack with his famous rushes up the ice. There was a moment of silence and then the Americans' star "Sweeney" Shriner quietly said, "with a rifle".[46]

At the end of the 1936-37 NHL hockey season Lionel stunned the sports world, announcing his retirement as an active player.

An indication of the reckless abandon that Lionel Conacher played the game of hockey can be best illustrated by this checklist of injuries he sustained during his career. Most notably, he received 600 stitches and endured having his nose broken 12 times!

In 1994, Conacher joined his brother Charlie as an Honoured Member of the Hockey Hall of Fame.

Retirement would not be a time for relaxation for the "Big

Train". In 1936 he announced that he was operating a new company called Conacher Construction Company. He further expanded his business portfolio when he purchased a portion of a brokerage firm and then invested in Alberta oil operations. Not satisfied with his wide-ranging commercial ventures, in 1937, Lionel added another job to his resume. He became a sports writer for the **Toronto Daily Star** commenting on the Canadian Football League. And, furthermore very few were aware that Lionel would soon be entering a new arena of competition!

He was convinced to enter the world of Canadian politics. His first foray into the political arena was to try and capture a seat in the Ontario Legislature for the Liberal Party. In his nomination speech, Lionel illustrated that his past would help him understand the needs of his constituency. Conacher said, "I believe I know the hardships some of the people are enduring at the present time, for I had them in my youth."[47] He ran in the usually Conservative riding of Bracondale and to the surprise of very few, he won. However, his margin of victory was by the slimmest of margins, a mere 37 votes.

One person who was certain that Lionel was well-suited to the world of politics was Tommy Gorman, who had served as general manager of both the Chicago Black Hawks and Montreal Maroons.

Gorman said, "Lionel Conacher will be just as successful in public life as he has been in sport....Conacher has wonderful natural executive ability and will prove a born leader in anything he undertakes."

The Maroons general manager went on to talk about Lionel's impact on that team. Gorman said, "…it was largely due to his (Conacher's) personal influence over the players and his grim determination and fearlessness on the ice that enabled the Maroons to make such stubborn fights for the championship."[48]

In the 1937 provincial election campaign, a newspaper story illustrated how Premier Mitchell Hepburn used Lionel's athletic ability to his best advantage. The situation occurred at a couple of campaign events in Galt and Kitchener. At the end of his speech, Hepburn realized that his exit was blocked by the throngs of supporters who were in attendance. That is until Conacher jumped into action.

> With Premier Hepburn close behind him, the smiling Conacher shouldered a pathway towards the exits. Crowds anxious to see the premier blocked the way. But Conacher's weight, gently but firmly applied, set aside all interference. The Big Train started towards open spaces and kept going. With Conacher running interference for him the premier found the going easy.[49]

In 1938 Lionel was appointed chairman of the Ontario Athletic Commission. But this was not the only sporting position that seemed to be opening up for the recently retired hockey star.

In September 1938 the sports pages of the Toronto newspapers trumpeted Lionel's possible return to the NHL, not as player or as a coach, but "from Montreal comes a despatch naming Lionel Conacher, M.L.A., as likely to be offered the position of Referee-in-Chief of the National Hockey League"[50].

As rumors about such postings and other news in the world of sport are quite common, the **Globe and Mail** reporter who wrote the story approached Conacher to verify the authenticity of the despatch. Lionel responded with the following information:

> I have been approached by several individual managers, but can't make a comment as to my own plans until I receive a definite offer. I feel sure that I could handle the job properly, and if the offer is sufficiently attractive, I would find it hard to refuse.[51]

Continuing, he said, "I do know that Canadiens, Black Hawks, Bruins, Rangers and Red Wings favour me…I haven't talked to Conny Smythe, but see no reason why he should object."[52]

But when the reporter asked Conn Smythe his opinion on Lionel becoming the Referee-in-Chief, his response was anything but positive. The owner of the Maple Leafs said, "They all favour Conacher, but with only seven clubs, I don't think there will be a Referee-in-Chief".[53]

It seems that perhaps it was only a rumour, or Mr. Smythe, as it was often intimated, really did wield a lot of power at the highest levels of the NHL! Whatever the situation, Lionel Conacher never became the NHL's Referee-in-Chief.

With the outbreak of World War Two, Lionel once again put his star power to use, travelling across the country establishing athletic programs for armed forces personnel. Squadron Leader Conacher's main responsibility was as sports director for the Royal Canadian Air Force. But his name and presence undoubtedly caused many a young Canadian to enlist in the Canadian armed forces.

All of his activities away from the Ontario Legislature, were not well-received by his constituents. As a result, he failed in his attempt for re-election. After the war, he was convinced to run for the Liberal Party in the 1945 federal election. But he lost. However, in 1949,[54] the voters of Toronto's Trinity riding elected him to Parliament. He was re-elected again in 1953 where he remained until his death in 1954.

In the 1949 federal election campaign, Lionel counted among the candidates challenging him for elected office, a rather unique opponent. Tim Buck was the long-serving secretary general of the Communist Party of Canada[55]. As the campaign progressed, the Communists, or Labour Progressives as they were more formally known at that time, must have felt that Conacher was the candidate to beat so they issued a circular attacking Lionel.

The political pamphlet charged that "Mr. Conacher did not

attend the legislature one single day when he was MPP for Bracondale in 1943." The **Toronto Star** was quick to point out that of course Conacher could not have attended to the Ontario Legislature because "he was in uniform" helping Canada's war effort.[56]

Buck's political propaganda piece also quoted a story in the **Globe and Mail** that claimed Lionel had said, "I drive anyone who doesn't agree with me out of the country." The **Toronto Star** corrected this story stating that the **Globe and Mail's** story actually said, "I would like to lead a group of Trinity people and not only run them out of our ballpark, but right out of the country." The **Star** went on to say that the combative Conacher was using the word "them" to refer to the Communists in the riding. Whether Buck's propaganda helped or hurt Lionel no one is really sure. But the Communist candidate was right about one thing, Conacher was the person to beat. But no one did! And Lionel was on his way to Ottawa and backbenches of the Liberal government under Prime Minister Louis St. Laurent.

Lionel also held another elected position at the same time as he was a member of the Canadian Parliament. In the early 1950s, until his death, Conacher held the office of the President of the NHL Old-Timers.

After the federal election, Lester Pearson, a government cabinet minister, and future Canadian Prime Minister, commented on the unique abilities of a particular group of three members of the Liberal government's backbenches. Mr. Pearson said,

> With Conacher, Dit Clapper and Bucko Macdonald in the House we will have the finest defence in parliamentary history. The leader of the opposition won't be able to stickhandle through and he's quite a stickhandler.[57]

Lionel Conacher was athletically active and competitive right to the end. In 1954 he died at the age of 53 playing softball on Parliament Hill. He collapsed after "legging out" a triple. For most people the hit would have been a single, but this was not the case for the ever-aggressive Conacher. With Tory MP Donald Fleming coming to bat and Lester Pearson, who was by all accounts a pretty good baseball player on deck, Lionel pushed it into high gear as he rounded first base and raced all the way to third where he collapsed.

The impact of his death was felt across the city of Toronto and beyond. More than 1,000 mourners crammed into St. John's Anglican Church on York Mills for his funeral. Mayor Lamport ordered all flags in the City of Toronto to fly at half-mast in tribute to a great athlete and great Torontonian.

A year after his brother's death, Charlie inaugurated a trophy in Lionel's name. The Conacher Memorial Trophy was initiated to be presented each year to the Ontario Lacrosse Association's Senior Championship team.[58] Lionel always excelled at lacrosse. He was inducted as a charter member of the Canadian Lacrosse Hall of Fame.

One of the other charter member inductees with Conacher was former Montreal Canadiens star and Hockey Hall of Fame member, "Newsy" Lalonde.

Each year since 1932 the Canadian Press (CP) takes a poll to determine Canada's top athlete. In 1978 the award given to Canada's Athlete of the Year, was re-named the Lionel Conacher Award. Ironically, Lionel never won this award during his athletic career. Of course, he did receive this accolade in 1950 when he was named the Athlete of the First Half Century.

Conacher's impact on other hockey players extended beyond his playing days. In December 1963, Gordie Howe was named Canada's top athlete of the year. The always humble Howe, who most hockey fans consider to be one of the top two or three players in the history of the sport, said that Lionel Conacher had always been "something of an idol in my eyes"[59].

Lionel Conacher Park is a small park near Yonge Street and St. Clair Avenue West that features a baseball diamond, a wading pool and a children's playground.

Lionel Conacher's wide-ranging sporting exploits led to his induction into the Canadian Sports Hall of Fame in 1994. With all of his accomplishments in the field of athletic endeavours, it is easy to see why he was named Canada's Athlete of the First Half Century in 1950.

In 1999, voting was held to select Canada's Athlete of the Twentieth Century. Many people thought that Lionel would be a logical choice. However, when the tallies were counted it was evident the voters thought differently, and three hockey superstars, Wayne Gretzky, Gordie Howe and Bobby Orr, all finished ahead of the fourth place Conacher.

When it was public knowledge that it was Gretzky, and not Conacher, who had been honoured as the Athlete of the Century, the **Toronto Star** voiced some dismay at this decision saying:

> The great Lionel Conacher was voted Canada's best athlete of the first 50 years of this century. He has since been surpassed, voters say, by Wayne Gretzky, Gordie Howe and Bobby Orr.
>
> Did all those responding to the poll know that Conacher did everything and did it well?
>
> There is no video footage to show them that on the same day he won a Grey Cup with the Argonauts, he played senior hockey when that league was one notch below the NHL.
>
> …Perhaps a footnote should be added: As voted by those who had actually seen most, if not all of the other candidates.[60]

Lionel Conacher and Carl Voss are the only two athletes to win both the Grey Cup and the Stanley Cup.

Lionel's successes have often been measured by his

performances on the various athletic fields of competition in which he participated; by his entrepreneurial endeavours; and of course his life in the world of Canadian politics. But it is certain that one could also measure his accomplishments in terms of the life he was able to provide for his family.

He was the father of five children. Two daughters, Constance and Diane, arrived first on the scene. Then in 1936, the **Toronto Daily Star** announced "there is a little "Big Train" in the Lionel Conacher family".[61]

The little "Big Train" was 9.5 pound Lionel Conacher Jr., and there would be two more boys to follow, David and Brian.

Lionel often said, "We'll take the cuts and the bruises so our kids can get an education".[62] Although he and his siblings attended Jesse Ketchum Public School and, he later attended university, Lionel's public school days ended at Grade Eight. His children would have a very different educational upbringing. Lionel Jr. and his sisters attended Baron Renfrew Public School in York Mills for a time before they and their younger brothers headed off to private school. The girls attended Havergal College and the boys were enrolled at Upper Canada College.

Like their father, the children were all involved in athletics. Some of their successes can be found in the pages of various Toronto newspapers.

Lionel Jr. and Diane, children of Lionel Conacher, former great Canadian athlete, captured championships yesterday at the annual sports day of Baron Renfrew Public School, York Mills.

Lionel won top honours in the junior boys division with 15 points. Diane headed all the senior girls with 18 points.[63]

After he moved on to Upper Canada College, Lionel Jr., continued to dominate the school sporting events that he entered. In 1951, at the UCC annual track and field meet he "won five junior events and set records in three of them".[64]

Lionel Jr. showed early on that he shared his father's ability for the game of football. A 1954 **Toronto Daily Star** article described the younger Conacher's exploits as a footballer with Upper Canada College. In a game against their rivals from Trinity College, the younger Conacher was called a "Big Train". The story said in part:

> In the second frame, with the score tied, Conacher waged a one-man war with the Trinity wall and climaxed a 60-yard touchdown march with a 15-yard run around end.[65]

Lionel Jr. continued to hone his football skills in school and he was rewarded for his efforts in the 1959 Canadian Football League Draft when he was selected by Montreal Alouettes.

Not to be outdone by his older brother, David Conacher, a

225-pound tackle, also made a mark for himself on the gridiron. In 1961 he earned a tryout with his father's old team the Argonauts, causing speculation in the media of the possibility of another Conacher making his way onto the Toronto football scene. Sports writer Jim Hunt wrote, "Don't be surprised if Argos have a Conacher in their lineup this season." And to support this claim, Hunt penned, "He's supposed to be able to beat his brother in a foot race which makes Dave a pretty rapid lineman."[66]

However, David's football career was short-lived. He would become an avid canoeist, kayaker and outdoorsman. He was a staunch supporter of the camping movement which was more than evident from the fact that it was requested that the Taylor Statten Camping Bursary Fund be a recipient of donations in lieu of flowers at his death. David died at the age of 73 in a kayaking accident on the Saguenay River on August 23, 2013.

Not to be outdone on the football field by his older brothers, Brian, the youngest of Lionel Conacher's five children, also loved to play football. But as you will see in Chapter 6, Brian's skills included football at the high school and university levels, but he is more noted for his abilities on the ice in the world of amateur and professional hockey.

Chapter Three

<u>Charlie Conacher</u>

Charlie Conacher is a member of the Hockey Hall of Fame and the Canadian Sports Hall of Fame. In the world of Canadian sports, Charlie is often over-shadowed by his older brother Lionel who was considered to be an outstanding all-around athlete. But, in terms of the game of hockey, it is generally conceded that Charlie was the better hockey player.

Charlie Conacher is a folk hero, especially with Toronto Maple Leaf hockcy fans. Born December 20, 1909, the sixth of ten children, it was never expected that he would become a superstar in the world of professional hockey. In fact, his hockey skills were so limited, the thought of Charlie even signing a contract to play professionally probably never crossed the minds of even his very best friends, or his family.

As a youngster, Charlie was not a great skater, perhaps not even a good skater. Consequently, when he played hockey with the other kids in the neighbourhood, Conacher often found himself confined to the role of goaltender. And, that is probably how things would have unfolded for the youngster, had it not been for Lionel.

Here is where the impact of his elder sibling came to play on the Charlie's destiny. When Lionel signed a professional hockey contract with the Pittsburgh Pirates. Charlie was 15 years old. Seeing that it was indeed possible to earn a good living playing hockey, Charlie decided that he too would become a professional hockey player. Speaking later in life, he described the value he and his siblings placed upon playing professional hockey:

> "We didn't have a penny as kids," Charlie once said. "But we knew that hockey could bring us something better in life, and Jesse Ketchum was where we learned the game. It was a hell of a lot of fun on that ice, but I'd be lying if I didn't say the money that us Conachers hoped to make one day was a big motivation.[67]

Today most "hockey authorities" suggest that the process of becoming a professional must begin when a player is very young. Many of these "experts" would consider that it would be impossible for a 15-year-old possessing very limited hockey skills to develop the level of his game to the extent that he could make it to professional hockey, especially the National Hockey League! But Charlie Conacher, like his brother Lionel before him, would prove this theory wrong!

Lionel had not learned to skate until he was 16 years old. Realizing that his skating skills were extremely lacking, like his brother, Charlie, at the age of 15, began to work very hard to improve his skating abilities and to hone the rest of his hockey talents. He told a friend, "I worked on my skating until I thought my legs would drop off."[68]

It was not long before Charlie's efforts began to bear fruit. Within two years, at the age of 17, he was playing organized hockey at a high level. He split the 1926-27 hockey season between the North Toronto OHA Senior team and the North Toronto OHA Junior squad. The next season (1927-28) Charlie became a member of one of Canada's most storied junior hockey franchises, the Toronto Marlboros.

As a member of the Marlboros, Charlie continued his hard work. It seemed like he had an "insatiable urge for practicing" and recounted how the eager youngster, "...haunted Claude Harris, the Marlboro goalie, until he agreed to stay after each official practice. Then Charlie would skate hard up the ice, and weave and stick-handle his way through a dozen invisible defencemen to make his shot on goal."[69]

It would be the tremendous successes of the 1928-29 hockey season that would bring Charlie's outstanding hockey abilities to the attention of Toronto hockey fans.

Using his drive and determination, not to mention, his booming shot, Charlie led the Marlboros' OHA Junior loop in scoring with 18 goals and total points with 21. What makes these numbers more significant is that he accumulated these scoring statistics in only eight games! As if to show the hockey world that his regular season scoring statistics had not been a fluke, Conacher led the Canadian Junior hockey playoffs in scoring and total points. His 24 goals in only 13 playoff games were a major reason that the Marlies captured the Memorial Cup, the symbol of Canadian Junior Hockey supremacy!

Charlie's scoring prowess was a major factor for the Toronto junior team's success in the eastern Canadian playoffs. After a 4-3 loss to the Ottawa Shamrocks in the first game of the Eastern finals, the Marlies had their backs to the wall. In the second game of the two-game total-points series for the right to go to the Memorial Championships, the Marlies roared back to a 3-1 victory to clinch the title by 6-5 total goals. The Marlies victory was achieved on the back of Charlie Conacher who scored all three Toronto goals![70]

Fans were not the only ones who were impressed by Charlie's hockey feats. On October 1, 1929, Conn Smythe, the owner and general manager of the Toronto Maple Leafs, inked the young Conacher to a professional contract for the 1929-30 hockey season. Ironically, Conacher signed his contract with the Leafs just four weeks before the stock market crash on October 29, 1929 which signalled the beginning of the Great Depression!

As part of his professional contract, Smythe gave Charlie a signing bonus of $2,000. Now, that may not seem like a lot of money when one considers the bonuses and salaries that professional athletes receive today, but in that era the amount was quite acceptable. However, the signing bonus did not impress big brother Lionel.

The Leaf owner paid the $2,000 bonus to Charlie in two dollar bills and according to Brian Conacher, his father Lionel, was not impressed by this action. He recalled, "...my father resented Connie doing this, and while he came to respect him more, later in life, I don't think he ever forgave him."[71]

Whatever reason Smythe had for paying Conacher his signing bonus entirely in two dollar bills, it would not be long before Charlie would be held in the highest esteem not only by the ownership of the Leafs, but also the fans of the "blue and white".

He became one of a very few players to score his first NHL goal in his first game, on his first shift. "He jumped on the ice, sailed down his right wing, took a pass from Eric Pettinger, walked around the defenceman and smoked a sizzler past Charlie Gardiner – his first goal in his first chance as a pro."[72]

In his rookie season in the NHL, Charlie Conacher notched 20 goals in 38 games. Today this may not seem like a significant goal scoring tally for a season, but in the 1930s, the NHL was a close-checking and low-scoring league. This style of hockey combined with the fact that the NHL season consisted of only 44 games meant that very few players reached the 20 goal plateau each season.

During his rookie campaign, a decision was made that would have an impact on the success of the Leafs, and at the same time, leave a mark on the history of the franchise that would be etched in the minds of Toronto fans for decades to come.

At the start of the season Charlie played on a line with centerman Joe Primeau and left winger Harold "Baldy" Cotton. But, when the team struggled, Conn Smythe did what many coaches and general managers do in that situation, he started to experiment with various line combinations. At one point during a game, Smythe inserted Charlie's former Marlboro team mate, Harvey Jackson[73], on the left wing with Primeau and Conacher. At first, this move appeared to have been a "one-time" experiment, as the trio did not remain together at that point in time. However, later, on December 29, 1929, Smythe, probably recalling the earlier experiment with the trio, deemed that it was time to put them together on a permanent basis.

The Primeau-Jackson-Conacher line was a hit with the fans and the media, but probably not the league's goaltenders, as they became a potent scoring threat whenever they were on the ice. Almost immediately, sportswriters started calling them the "Kid Line"[74]. This moniker would stick with them until Primeau retired at the end of the 1935-36 hockey season. However, the mark this threesome made on Toronto Maple Leafs history, and in fact, the annals of the entire NHL, would make them one of the most celebrated forward lines in the history of the league.

What made the "Kid Line" so effective? Well, there are lots of reasons. In an article about a 1950's Leaf forward line featuring Bob Pulford and Brian and Barry Cullen, written two decades after the vaunted trio had ceased playing as a unit, it was revealed how the "Kid Line" had prepared. The article said that during practice, Conacher, Primeau and Jackson would "pass the puck back and forth at all speeds until each man knew just what kind of passes to expect from the others and knew when to expect them."[75]

At the end of his rookie season, in the summer of 1930, Charlie was faced with a huge decision. The result of which could mean the end of his hockey career!

His decision was predicated by an event that had occurred ten years earlier, when Charlie had been a rambunctious 10-year-old ready to take on any challenge. One day he was climbing the iron beams that supported the Huntley Street Bridge. The would-be "mountain climber" lost his balance and fell thirty or forty feet. Fortunately, he landed on the top branches of a pine tree. The tree appeared to have broken his fall and saved him from serious injury, or even death.

For some reason, internal damages from the fall had not been discovered. In the summer of 1930, it appeared that the fall of a decade earlier had indeed left its mark on Conacher's internal organs. It was determined that he needed to have a kidney removed. After the surgery, the doctors were no doubt surprised when Charlie told them that he planned on playing hockey again. Author Ron McAllister recounted that the doctors warned him about returning to hockey saying, "If you do, young man, we can't be responsible."[76]

Despite the admonitions of the doctors, Charlie returned to the NHL. Probably the opposition goaltenders had wished that Conacher had listened to his medical advisers because in the next two seasons he blossomed even more as a potent goal scorer, leading the NHL in goals with 31 in 1930-31 and 34 markers in 1931-32.

In his second season in the NHL, Charlie and Lionel were becoming frequent topics of discussion in the Toronto sports media. Sometimes the stories were true, and others times they were more fanciful. The brothers became the focal point of what could best be described as a "once in a lifetime" situation. Actually the event may have been even rarer than that!

What happened? Lionel assisted on a goal by his brother Charlie. Now there is nothing unique about a brother assisting on another brother's goal. Except on that occasion, they were playing on two different teams! A check with the NHL's statistics department revealed that the story was more fanciful than factual as no assist was ever recorded.

This farfetched tale found its origin in a game between Charlie's Maple Leafs and Lionel's Montreal Maroons.

Charlie beat the Maroon defence on Lionel's side and was bearing down on "Flat" Walsh (the Maroons' goalie), when Lionel suddenly wheeled about, tripped over himself, and sent his stick flying in Charlie's direction, spoiling the latter's chance for shooting. Immediately Referee Bert Corbeau faced the puck off at centre ice, awarding a goal to the Toronto club in Charlie's favour and the assist came from his big brother.[77]

Like the other members of his family, Charlie was an able athlete in more than one sport. For instance, in 1931 he showed off his golfing skills by capturing the club championship at the Port Colborne golf club.[78]

The 1931-32 hockey season would mark a new era in the history of professional hockey in Toronto. The Leafs opened their season in a brand new arena, Maple Leaf Gardens. When one considers the economic constraints the country was enduring at that time with large numbers of people lining up each and every day at "bread lines" hoping to provide some form of sustenance for themselves and their families, the Maple Leafs were going to have to do something to attract fans to buy tickets to the games. After all, the team not only had to pay their players' salaries, but they also had to pay for the new arena that had just been built!

The answer to this economic dilemma just might have been the kid from Scollard Street! Charlie Conacher had a flair for the dramatic. And the 1931-32 season he would provide plenty of evidence of his knack for the spectacular. The night Maple Leaf Gardens opened, the Leafs lost 2-1 to Chicago, but the first Maple Leaf player to score on their new home rink was Charlie Conacher[79].

On January 19, 1932, Charlie continued his impressive play, becoming the first Maple Leaf to score five goals in one game as the Leafs dominated the New York Americans by an 11-3 score. Ironically, the New York goalie that evening, Roy Worters, was a long-time friend of the Conacher family, and would become a business partner with Charlie in their post-NHL careers.

The magic moments for Conacher continued a couple of weeks later on February 6, 1932 when he notched the fastest game-winning goal in the history of the NHL when he scored at the six second mark of the first period of a 6-0 victory over the Boston Bruins.

Toronto finished the 1931-32 season in third place, but behind a play-off leading six-goal performance by Charlie Conacher, the Maple Leafs captured their first Stanley Cup!

When the playoffs began, the Rangers were overwhelming favourites to defeat the young Toronto team. Because New York's home rink, Madison Square Gardens, had been booked for the circus that came to the "Big Apple" every spring, the Rangers would only have the luxury of one home game in the final series.

The first game was played in New York, the second would be in Boston, and the rest of the series would be contested at Maple Leaf Gardens. Given that the opening game would be their last with home ice advantage the Rangers were looking for a victory.

With the score tied 1-1, the Kid Line, stepped to the fore for the Leafs, Busher Jackson netted three markers and Charlie Conacher banged home another with a howitzer shot, and the score was 5-1 in favour of the visitors. But, by early in the third period the New Yorkers had made a match of it by scoring three times. And then, as they mounted a continuous barrage in the Maple Leafs' end of the ice, goalie, Lorne Chabot, changed with flow of the game took things into his own hands.

The Leaf goalie "smothered the puck, dove to the ice and began fumbling with the strap on one of his leg pads. He created a delay that lasted long enough to give the Leafs the 'breather" they required. When play resumed they had steadied down, they handcuffed Ranger attempts to apply their power attack…"[80] And, to solidify their victory Leaf forward "Busher" Jackson set up Red Horner, for the Leafs sixth goal and the game was essentially over.

The teams headed to Boston for Game Two. Hoping to erase the bad taste of their loss in the first game, the Rangers roared to a 2-0 lead. But, as in the previous game, it was the Kid Line that issued the Leafs' response, Jackson and Conacher quickly tied the score. The rest of the Toronto players, eager to participate in the scoring, pushed for more markers. Conacher netted his second of the game and Clancy popped in two, and Cotton notched another and the game ended 6-2.

Game Three proved to be the clincher as the Leafs captured their first Stanley Cup in the first-ever sweep of a final series. However, the game had a dramatic moment that had the entire crowd on the edge of its seats. It involved Charlie Conacher and his powerful shot.

> From just inside the blue-line, Conacher let go a drive that caught Goalie Roach under the heart. The impact drove Roach back into the nets but he straightened up and cleared the puck. Then slowly he dropped his stick, struggled a second with his gloved hands at his throat, and slumped to the ice.

> An awed silence settled over the arena as Roach stiffened out. It looked as if he had been instantly killed. He lay without a move, and there were moments of anxiety before the little goalie responded. It took him five minutes to get over the shock of the blow. But he stayed in there, game as they come, and he was given a tremendous ovation.[81]

Only a few days after winning the Stanley Cup, the **Toronto Daily Star** reported that one of the city's hockey heroes was still a kid at heart. It was reported that the Chief Coroner, Dr. M.M. Crawford, was driving along Macpherson Ave., when his route was blocked by a group of youngsters playing road hockey. The article reported that:

> One of the players was a huge two hundred pounder and the rest of the laughing youngsters seemed to be picking on him. He was the target of all the attacks. The big fellow was Charlie "Big Shot" Conacher and the neighbourhood kids were having the time of their life playing with their hockey hero.[82]

1932 would continue to provide Charlie with some great moments. On July 29th of that year his son, Charles William Conacher Jr., or as he came to be known, Pete Conacher, was born. Charlie's son would continue the Conacher tradition of great athleticism, carving out a six-season career in the NHL, largely with the Chicago Black Hawks and the New York Rangers.

Charlie was more than a goal scorer, he proved that he was pretty good at stopping goals as well. Dick Irvin, in his book, **In the Crease: Goaltenders Look at Life in the NHL**, wrote that in the 1930s "...if a goalie was hurt late in a period a forward or a defenceman would take over, minus goaltending equipment save for the stick and maybe the gloves... (In 1933) Charlie Conacher, one of the greatest goal scorers of his day, played goal in three different games for a total of nine minutes and didn't allow a goal."[83]

> By 1933, Charlie Conacher "became Canada's first coast-to-coast sports idol, No Gallup Poll produced Charlie as the

Nation's Choice. The popularity barometer was a 'send in a label and get a picture of your favorite hockey star' Campaign inaugurated by 'Bee-Hive' Corn Syrup directors. The labels poured in by the thousands. The picture most requested was of Conacher.

Conacher, on and off the ice, was certainly one of the most colorful personalities to ever come down the hockey pike....

Conacher's craze for speed was actually an obsession. On the ice he was one of the fastest men from the blueline in – the stamp of a great player – that the game had ever known. He seemed to take-off, jet propelled, and it was this characteristic that engendered so many of his injuries.[84]

The next season, 1934-35, Conacher notched 36 goals to lead the NHL in scoring. But, he again also played goal on one occasion. When goalie George Hainsworth was injured and forced to seek repairs in the dressing room, Charlie agreed to tend the Leafs net. He refused to put on the goalie pads, saying with bravado, "Just gimme his goal stick and I'll shut 'em out."[85] And that is what he did, giving his adoring fans another reason to cheer for him.

Charlie enjoyed playing other sports besides hockey, a 1933 newspaper article reported that the younger Conacher was hoping to suit up with Lionel's professional football team. But the reporter mused about the possibility of this actually happening, remembering a time when Charlie had wished to play professional lacrosse:

We wonder what the big guns of the Maple Leaf Hockey Club will say about Charlie's football activities. The husky right winger would have played professional lacrosse two summers ago, had it not been for the objection raised by the hockey boss.[86]

Conacher's goal scoring and flair for the dramatic, made him not only popular with hockey fans, but also a favourite of Leaf owner Conn Smythe. In fact, Charlie and George Armstrong are the only two Toronto Maple Leafs that Conn Smythe named a horse after.[87]

Ironically, later in life Smythe came to loathe Charlie. Some suggest that this change in attitude was essentially due to Conacher's off-ice activities. Still, others suggest that it was Charlie's campaign, along with the support of sports reporter Dick Beddoes, to help induct his long-time friend "Busher" Jackson into the Hockey Hall of Fame that ignited Smythe's wrath towards Charlie.

Conn Smythe's Memoirs, **Conn Smythe: If You Can't Beat 'Em in the Alley**, written in 1981, with Scott Young, paints a picture of Charlie Conacher that is hardly flattering.

For instance, at one point in his memoirs, Smythe describes how he felt about Conacher's and "Busher" Jackson's roles on the Leafs illustrious "Kid Line", with center Joe Primeau:

The famous Kid Line was born. But I must say right here that for all the goals they got and all-star teams they were on, Conacher and Jackson were never half as good players as they were thought to be. They wanted Joe to do all the work, and they'd score the goals.[88]

Conacher led the league with 31 goals and the "Kid Line" scored 58 of the 118 goals the team scored all season. But the line failed to score a single goal when the Leafs were eliminated by Chicago in the first round of the playoffs, Smythe laid the reason for the team's defeat rather harshly at the feet of Charlie and "Busher" saying, "Conacher and Jackson never did feel very interested in getting in shape. They were too busy driving their fast cars and chasing women."[89]

Charlie, did indeed like fast cars. Author Ed Fitkin described this need for speed, both on and off the ice, in his book, **The Gashouse Gang of Hockey**,

> Away from the rink Charlie was noted for the almost demoniacal way he drove a car. He had cream-colored roadster that was his pride and joy because it literally could fly along the highways. Conn Smythe used to say that he'd be driving to the Leaf training camp - either at St. Catharines or Galt or Preston – and Conacher would swoosh past him, tooting raucously, en route to Toronto; and before Smythe reached his destination Conacher would pass him on the way back.[90]

Smythe continued his negative statements about Conacher saying, "I should have broken up the Kid Line around 1935 or so. I didn't have the guts. Of course, they were a big gate attraction. I could have found lots of wingers to go with Joe Primeau, but he was the only centre who could make Conacher and Jackson click."[91]

After Primeau retired, Smythe described further his thinking about a replacement center for the "Kid Line" saying:

I briefly tried Apps between Conacher and Jackson, but that didn't work at all. Those two had to have someone like Joe doing all their lifting for them. I wasn't going to sacrifice the Apps talent to work like Primeau had, to make stars out of two other guys.[92]

One can only wonder how much truth there is in these comments by Conn Smythe. It certainly seems to challenge the popular thought about the greatness of Charlie Conacher!

Early in his hockey career the popular Conacher was tagged with the moniker, the "Big Bomber".

Although many suggest that this nickname was essentially due to his booming shoot. One could reasonably argue that the way he played the game was why he earned the title of the "Big Bomber"!

Standing over six feet tall and weighing around 200 pounds, Charlie was a big man for that era of the NHL. One acquaintance said of Conacher's style of play, "the trouble with Big Charlie is, he thinks he's a truck, so he takes on the other team in a personal, hand-to-hand battle!"[93]

When Charlie first entered the NHL, he was quickly accepted by the veterans around the league.

What amazed the veterans was the fact that 20-year-old Conacher not only could take it but he could dish it out, as well. They began to treat him with a respect seldom before afforded a newcomer.[94]

Team mate, and long-time member of the Maple Leaf organization, King Clancy once said, "He was my protection as a Maple Leaf....Conacher was Toronto's policeman for many years and a great one. He didn't go looking for trouble, but if it came along he would clear it up."[95]

It could never be stated that he let blood lines interfere when it came to defending a teammate. On one occasion, Charlie took exception to his brother, Lionel's treatment of another Maple Leaf player. After the dust settled from the battle between the Conacher brothers, Charlie said, "Nobody messes with my teammates...Not even my brother."[96]

Charlie Conacher was more than a fighter, he was also a prolific goal scorer. Once again it is quote from King Clancy that pays testament to the impact of the explosiveness of Charlie's shot.

On one occasion Conacher had tried a shot at the goaltender, only to miss and hit his team mate Clancy in the rear end causing Clancy to recall, "I felt like somebody had turned a blow torch on me. I couldn't sit down for a week."[97]

Simply put, "Big Charlie could crack a 2-inch plank with the fury of his shot! Hockey was work to him, and he went at it like a sledge-hammer."[98]

After a goal-scoring letdown in the 1932-33 hockey season when he netted only 14 goals, Conacher found his old form as public enemy number one with the league's goalies. He terrorized the netminders for the following three NHL campaigns leading the league in goal-scoring three straight seasons and winning the league scoring title twice. His popularity with the Leaf fans was unparalleled at that time. Long-time sports columnist Damien Cox, and one-time Leaf general manager Gord Stellick, called Conacher arguably the most dashing player to ever play for the Leafs.[99]

Hockey fans of all ages love to wear the jersey of their favourite sports stars. Today, it is not surprising to see fans attending hockey games, wearing the jersey of their favourite team, and often more specifically the number of their favourite player. At the same time, it is common place to see youngsters wearing jerseys featuring their favourite team or the hockey hero while playing hockey on backyard rinks or playing ball hockey in school yards and parking lots. Even during the harsh economic times of the 1930s, fans adored their sports heroes in a similar fashion. And in Toronto, Maple Leaf players, especially Charlie Conacher, were idolized.

Perhaps one of the reasons for his popularity was due to Foster Hewitt's radio broadcasts of Maple Leaf hockey games from coast-to-coast. In the midst of the hard times being endured by hockey fans in the depression that was the wreaking havoc on the Canadian economic landscape, Charlie Conacher must have been seen by many as a beacon of hope. After all, his own experience of growing up in poverty conditions were well-known. Many fans probably identified with Charlie and perhaps even tucked away in their heart the hope that they, too, could follow in his footsteps to success.

Charlie once stated that "I was born in one of Toronto's high-class slums. We didn't have a pretzel, we didn't have enough money to buy toothpaste."[100]

Red Burnett, the long-time sports writer for the **Toronto Star** said of Conacher "This was my Conacher, leader and champion of the poor sweats who knew what it was to be hungry and without a dime."[101]

Ironically, one youngster who worshipped Charlie and, who would later in life, become the object of the affection of Toronto fans himself, was Ted Kennedy. As a youngster, Ted "Teeder" Kennedy[102], idolized Charlie Conacher.

When he played hockey as a youngster Kennedy always wore Conacher's #9 jersey. However, when Kennedy joined the Leafs, he was unable to continue his tradition of honouring his hockey hero. At the time of his arrival to the Leafs his favourite number was worn by veteran Lorne Carr. However his disappointment would be short-lived.

> When Carr retired after the playoffs of 1946, the Maple Leafs decided that Kennedy finally should have the opportunity to wear number 9. At the next season's opening game, Charlie Conacher made a special on-ice appearance to present his old number to the beaming youngster.[103]

It was not only the youngsters who hero-worshipped Charlie Conacher. It was often said by his friends that "...if Foster Hewitt ever had a hero, it was Charlie Conacher."[104]

Charlie and Foster ultimately became good friends. This was a friendship that lasted long after Charlie left the game of professional hockey. Of this friendship, Scott Young wrote,

> Conacher later made a fortune from good investments, often passed along to him by hockey fans. Some of the tips he shared with Foster.[105]

Charlie was not the only Conacher to assist Foster Hewitt in his economic pursuits. In 1945, Lionel used his influence within the Liberal Party to convince Federal cabinet minister C.D. Howe to grant Foster a licence for his new radio station CKFH.[106]

Charlie's team mates also adored him. He was not only a great goal scorer and a defender of his team mates when the going got tough, but he was also one of the guys who kept the locker room smiling. He loved to tease his team mates and was a real jokester.

Many years ago "Ace" Bailey told a great story about Charlie and his team mate Alex Levinsky. It seems that after most games, Conacher would collect money and food orders from the Maple Leaf players and head to a local deli for sandwiches and to another local "retailer" for some beer. When he returned with the sandwiches and beer, after rummaging through the bag of sandwiches, he would tell Levinsky (who was Jewish) that he couldn't find Alex's sandwich. Not wanting to eat a non-kosher sandwich, Levinsky would settle for a bottle of beer, or two, instead. At some point, much to the delight of the entire team, including Levinsky, Charlie would dramatically proclaim "Oh look, Alex, I found your sandwich!" According to Bailey, Conacher and Levinsky would go through this charade

78

several times a season and the humour of it all never tired on them or their team mates.[107]

> Conacher was a man apart. He hated training and he had an intense dislike for too-rigid discipline. He did much as he pleased. He was the high man on the Toronto totem pole, the scoring ace, the big drawing card for fandom. Big, boisterous, bombastic Charlie went all-out in everything he did and he was the kind of a guy who would try anything once. He had a great zest for life and a great aptitude for deviltry.[108]

King Clancy, long-time member of the Maple Leaf organization, recalled that one of his favourite memories of Charlie occurred on March 17, 1933. The occasion was "King Clancy Night" at the Gardens. On this wonderful occasion, two of his teammates decided to play a trick on him. Clancy remembered that "Hap Day and Charlie Conacher – rubbed soot all over my face that night when the lights were turned out just before my big introduction".[109] With a soiled face the honoured Leaf had to skate out to be introduced to the crowd.

Another example of Conacher's stunts involving his fellow players occurred when "Charlie Conacher hung Ace Bailey by his feet out of a hotel window."[110]

It seems that Charlie liked to use his immense strength to hang people out of windows. Foster Hewitt recalled an incident involving Conacher and his roommate and family friend, "Baldy"

Cotton. The team was on a road trip to New York, when, for some reason Cotton locked Charlie out of their room. Conacher reacted by yelling "Lock me out, eh?" Then Foster said Charlie

> "…backed off down the hall and took dead aim at the door like William Tell sizing up that apple.
>
> Inside the room Cotton heard the loud clomp of hooves and here – keerash – came Conacher pile-driving his bulk against the door. The door lost.
>
> Then Conacher snatched Cotton fore and aft and held him, loosely, out the window. Cotton was so shy of heights that he blacked out putting the star on the Christmas tree. Now he fainted in Conacher's arms. Charlie was holding him only 22 storeys above the ground.[111]

Charlie Conacher was more than just an All-Star with the hockey fans, he was selected to the NHL First All-Star Team on three occasions, 1934[112], 1935 and 1936. And, he garnered Second Team honours twice, in 1932 and 1933.

He achieved all of these honours and accolades despite the fact that many of his hockey seasons were cut short because of a litany of injuries. Perhaps it was his hard-nosed style of play and unwillingness to take the easy route when he was driving towards the opposition's goal that caused him to miss so many games most seasons. A short-list of some his injuries include an infected hand in

1930; a broken hand in not one season, but three, 1931, 1932 and 1936. Charlie also suffered several shoulder dislocations[113]. Or, maybe it was the effects of having only one kidney that made him susceptible to missing hockey games. In the end, it was probably a combination of both of these factors that brought an end to his hockey career all too soon.

In the spring of 1936, Charlie Conacher's legend grew even larger! It all happened in a two-game-total-goal, play-off series between the Leafs and Boston Bruins.

The first game had been played in Boston and the Bruins had dumped the Leafs 3-0. At the opening face-off of the second game, the Leafs, and their fans, knew they had their backs to the wall. The team had 60 minutes to erase Boston's three-goal lead and then they had to add a winning marker.

What happened in this hockey game is what makes legends. Early in the game, the Bruins notched another goal and now the margin was four! It was at his point that Charlie Conacher took the team on his shoulders. When the game was over Conacher had scored a hat trick and added another assist to lead the Maple Leafs to a 5-4 total goals, play-off victory.[114]

Near the end of the 1936-37 hockey season, stories began to circulate that Charlie was considering retirement:

During the last visit of Toronto Leafs to Montreal, Charlie

Conacher told friends there that he was determined to retire at the end of the season.

He said that his literary duties, his gas station and some profitable ventures in mining stocks had placed him in such a position that he was independent of the rewards hockey had been bringing him.

Conacher has dropped hints during the early parts of this season to Toronto friends that he is weary of chasing pucks…"[115]

After playing only 19 games in the 1937-38 hockey season he suffered a wrist injury. After a thorough medical examination on January 20, 1938, Conacher retired.[116]

But, after some rest and relaxation in Florida, a re-invigorated and optimistic Conacher changed his retirement plans. But his days with the Maple Leafs were over. In October 1938 Charlie was traded to Detroit and was convinced to "un-retire" and play in the Motor City. After a less than stellar season in which he notched a paltry 8 goals, the Red Wings did not offer to renew his contract and Charlie's NHL rights were returned to Toronto.

However, his stay with his former team would be short. Before he could once again don his blue and white jersey, Charlie was dealt to the New York Americans. After two seasons on Broadway, Charlie Conacher retired as an active player in the NHL at the end of the 1940-41 NHL season.

He may have hung up is skates, but Charlie was not yet ready to leave the game. Before the start of the 1942-43 hockey season, he turned to coaching. Conacher's first stint behind the bench would be in Oshawa with the Junior "A" Generals. He coached in the OHA Junior "A" loop for five hockey seasons, leading his team to the Memorial Cup Championships in 1942, 1943 and, finally in 1944, Coach Conacher and the Generals on their third trip to Canadian Junior Hockey finals, captured the Memorial Cup.

His successful stint in junior hockey attracted the attention of the NHL's Chicago Black Hawks. He spent three seasons in the "Windy City" until he retired at the end of the 1949-50 hockey season. His last season in Chicago garnered him some attention of a different sort. He punched Lou Walter, a Detroit sportswriter, who brought a lawsuit against the Hawks coach. However, NHL President Clarence Campbell probably saved Conacher from the courts. The league's president fined Charlie $200 and demanded that he apologize to the scribe. This led to Walter dropping his legal actions.[117]

In Chicago one of his star players was his brother Roy who was a high-scoring left winger. Ironically, if Charlie had remained with the Black Hawks for another couple of seasons he would have had the opportunity to coach his son Pete, who debuted with Hawks in the 1951-52 NHL season.

Charlie parlayed his hockey career into a successful life after hockey in the world of business. In 1937, Conacher began writing a sports column in the **Globe and Mail** called "Conacher's Comment: Hockey Discussed by One of the Game's Greatest Players".

As it has been discussed elsewhere in this book, Charlie was more than a "one-sport" athlete. Among the other sports that he played at high levels of competition, football, lacrosse and softball were perhaps his other "best sports". In fact, in a story published in 1941 about the NHL Oldtimers playing a charity softball game in Huntsville, revealed that Charlie Conacher "would have been one of the best modern softballers had he not beckoned to professional hockey's call."[118]

He owned several businesses including the Conroy Hotel, located at the corner of Dufferin Street and Lawrence Avenue in north Toronto, with long-time family friend, former NHL goalie Roy Worters.

Bert Conacher recalled that he and his twin brother Roy worked for Charlie at the Conroy. He recollected one of the reasons for the success of the hotel, "With no other beverage room for miles around, the Conroy enjoyed the biggest beer sales in Toronto."[119]

Conacher owned a popular dance hall known as the Dardenella at Wasaga Beach. Some of his other very important business connections included his association with oil and gas magnates Max Bell and Frank McMahon, who were involved in developing the Turner Valley[120] in the Province of Alberta. He made many other shrewd investments including a very successful gas station at the corner of Yonge Street and Davenport Road, which he owned with his brother Lionel.

It was suggested that Charlie and Lionel did more than serve gasoline from their gas station. Sports historians James Duplacey and Charles Wilkins in **Forever Rivals** submit that "During the Depression, Conacher and his brother Lionel ran a bootlegging operation above a Toronto garage"[121].

Charlie also became a long-time friend of Hollywood legend Bing Crosby.[122]

Always the promoter, Charlie garnered publicity when the Beatles were signed to perform at Maple Leaf Gardens. He was quoted as saying "Never mind the Leafs, get me some Beatles tickets."[123]

In the 1960s Charlie was stricken with cancer. Never one, to let something like cancer get him down, Charlie attended his nephew Brian Conacher's wedding, looking dashing in his white suit only a few months before he passed away due to cancer on December 30, 1967"[124]at 58 years of age.

Charlie Conacher's impact on his friends continued well-past his death. For many years fund-raising events were held to further research into laryngeal (throat) cancer. The results of the efforts of his friends culminated in 1985 when Toronto General Hospital was endowed with $4 million to create the Charlie Conacher Research Wing.[125][126]

The Charlie Conacher Humanitarian Award[127], also known as the Charlie Conacher Memorial Trophy, was given to the NHL player who was recognized for outstanding humanitarian service.[128]The award was first presented in 1969 when the recipient was long-time Toronto Maple Leaf captain George Armstrong. The last player to receive this honour was Calgary Flames forward Jim Peplinski in 1984.[129]

Chapter Four

<u>Roy and Bert Conacher</u>

In 1915, not one, but two more Conachers entered the world. Like their older siblings, twins Roy and Bert Conacher would hone their athletic abilities on the playground of Jesse Ketchum Public School. Not surprisingly by the time they were teenagers, the youngest boys of the Conacher clan were being touted for their hockey skills and future potential as professional players. Even though they were twins, their hockey talents were very different. Roy was a smooth skating forward with an aptitude for outsmarting the opposition defenders to create scoring opportunities for himself and his teammates. Brother Bert, on the other hand, was an equally adept hockey player, only his skills were that of a heavy-hitting defenceman.

Unfortunately, at age 16, Bert's dreams of fulfilling his dreams of a professional hockey career came crashing to a sudden halt.

The devastating event happened innocently enough one day, when as usual, the Conachers and their friends were embroiled in a fiercely competitive game of road hockey. Bert, Roy, several of the neighbourhood kids, and even big brother Charlie, who was already a star with the hometown Maple Leafs, were the contestants in this game. These ball hockey games have been described as "ferocious road contests with sticks, a sponge ball, and empty coal sacks for the goalies' nets."[130]

Charlie and Bert were battling for the ball when Charlie's stick flew up and clipped Bert's face close to his left eye. At first, it looked like the usual type of minor injury incurred in a sporting activity. The wound was stitched and nothing more was thought of the event until about eight months later. It was at that time that Bert's vision started to fade. Over the course of time his vision was completely lost. Examinations to discover what had happened revealed that Charlie's stick had most likely nicked an optic nerve which resulted in the loss of vision.

Harold Ballard, who was the manager of the junior team that Bert played for, said that Conacher was "as talented as any of the hockey Conachers". This sentiment was shared by many others in the hockey world, including Jack Adams, the general manager of the Detroit Red Wings, and "Peanuts" O'Flaherty, an NHL scout.[131]

Although Charlie had been strongly influenced by his older brother Lionel with regards to hockey, it is probably unlikely that the oldest Conacher brother had more than a passing influence on Bert and Roy. Bert said that as a kid he really had no idea how good Lionel was as a hockey player, telling **Toronto Star** columnist George Gamester, "He (Lionel) was 16 years older than me."[132]

Bert played the defence position much like his older brother

88

Lionel. There are many newspaper accounts of games in which Conacher played a significant role providing his team with "some blue-line thumping".[133] And, like both of his older brothers, Bert was not afraid to drop the gloves and fight his opponents.

Although he played a physical game, the youngest Conacher also possessed a scoring touch. As a youngster playing in a low-scoring era, Bert often found a way to get his name etched on the game's score sheet. And, later, in the 1950s, when he suited up with his brothers for NHL Old-Timer exhibition games, he often was one of the scoring leaders in these highly competitive matches. For instance in an exhibition match played in Bracebridge, Bert banged home three goals and Charlie notched two markers. Ironically, big brother Lionel could only find his way onto the scoring stats that night with a lonely assist.

Bert may not have had many recollections of Lionel's hockey activities, but he did have some memories of Charlie's hockey exploits including the events surrounding the opening night at Maple Leaf Gardens. It seems that there was more than one Conacher at that game between the Leafs and Black Hawks that night. Bert remembered that Charlie was "on the ice and me and Roy selling programs in the stands".[134]

Like his older siblings, Bert Conacher was adept at many other sports. For instance, in 1936, when the Jesse Ketchum softball team beat an all-star team of former students including Bert and

Lionel, it was Bert who hit a home run to account for half of his team's effort in the losing cause.[135]

He was also an avid golfer. In 1966, he accomplished what every golfer dreams of doing. He recorded a hole-in-one while playing at the Brooklea club, near Midland Ontario. He holed out on the 140 yard, 18th hole using a 9-iron.[136]

Bert and Roy participated in many of the off-ice ventures of their older brothers. When Charlie and Lionel opened their BA gas station at Yonge Street and Davenport Road in Toronto, not far from their childhood home, Bert went to work for his older brothers. And, later when Charlie opened the Dardenella Dance club in Wasaga Beach, both Bert and Roy traveled to Wasaga Beach to help maintain that business. The twins followed big brother Charlie to the Conroy Hotel to help him run that north Toronto entertainment venue.

Bert continued to be active in sports such as charity "old timer" events and golf. He lived a long life until May 2014 when he passed away in his 98th year.

Roy Conacher

Roy Conacher is sometimes referred to as the "other Conacher". Despite his exceptional hockey skills and outstanding statistics, he is often ignored in favour of his older brothers, Lionel and Charlie. Perhaps he does not receive the recognition that he deserves because he spent most of his professional hockey career playing in Boston and Chicago, unlike Charlie and Lionel who spent many seasons playing in the Canadian hockey hotbeds of Toronto and Montreal.

This "Rodney Dangerfield" tag also happened even when he was starring for the Boston Bruins. Despite the fact that he was leading the league in goals and was a Stanley Cup hero, Roy's role, and that of his line mates, was often considered by both the fans and the media to be secondary to their more famous team mates, Milt Schmidt, Woody Dumart, and Bobby Bauer who played together on the "Kraut Line".

Roy Conacher's hockey skills were considered by many to be different than those of his two older brothers. First of all, Lionel was a defenceman and Roy was a smooth skating forward. And Charlie was best described as a power forward using his size and strength to bull his way toward the goalie's net, when he would unleash a thundering blast which made defenders unwilling to drop to their knees to block the shot. Whereas most hockey fans and "experts" of the day felt that Roy possessed a natural talent that depended more upon finesse to make his way to the net to score a goal. But, like his brother Charlie, Roy had a big shot. He was often described as "a left-handed forward with a rifle shot".[137]

This is not to suggest that this Conacher brother was smaller than his older siblings. In fact, size and physical attributes paid little impact on the differences between the brothers' hockey skills. Both Charlie and Roy were 6'1" tall, an inch shorter than Lionel. Charlie and Lionel tipped the scales at 195 to 200 pounds, which was 20 pounds more than their younger brother. These are hardly numbers to suggest that Roy was a little guy incapable of playing anything other than a finesse game.

His nephew, Brian, says, "From what I have heard, I think that Uncle Roy was probably the best hockey player in the family."[138]

As early as October 1935 the word about Roy Conacher's hockey prowess had extended beyond his hometown. At that time, he traveled to Saint John New Brunswick to participate in a training camp with the Boston Bruins. It was rumored that he would be signed to play for the Bruins' development team, the Boston Cubs, for further seasoning.[139] But instead, Roy returned to Toronto to play junior hockey.

His hockey talents were abundantly evident throughout his amateur career. In the 1935-36 season Roy led the league in goal scoring. In the team's 12 game playoff run to the Memorial Cup

Championship he led the West Toronto Nationals to the Canadian junior hockey title with 8 goals and 5 assists.[140]

After his outstanding junior career came to such a successful conclusion Conacher moved on the OHA Senior "A" league playing for the Toronto Dominions. His team enjoyed a long run in the 1936-37 Allan Cup play downs before losing to the Sudbury Frood Tigers in the Eastern Canadian Senior Hockey Final series. Conacher did his best to lead his team to victory and stave off elimination.

> Led by lanky Roy Conacher, Toronto Dominions jumped back into the Allan Cup race at Maple Leaf Gardens last night....
>
> Conacher, younger brother of Charlie and Lionel of professional hockey fame, gunned three of the four markers for the Happy Day – Harold Ballard crew, his last coming on a penalty shot in the third period.[141]

It has been often claimed that Roy was at first reticent to make professional hockey his career. Whether this is true or not it has been said that Lionel and Charlie both actively encouraged him to turn pro. And, on October 23, 1938 he followed their urging and inked a professional contract with the Boston Bruins for the 1938-39 NHL season.

Roy's rookie debut in the NHL was auspicious to say the least. He notched 26 goals in the regular season. The rookie's season total for goals not only led the Bruins, but the entire NHL! His goal production was not without some historic moments. Roy Conacher equalled "the season's goal-getting record of four tallies for a game".[142]

Despite his great goal scoring numbers, when it came time for the NHL to choose its top rookie, Roy would have settle for second place in the voting. He lost the Calder Trophy by a mere 4 points to his teammate, goaltender Frankie Brimsek.[143]

His scoring productivity continued in the Stanley Cup playoffs that year, notching 6 goals and 4 assists. Behind his scoring prowess the Bruins brought home the Stanley Cup.

It was during the Bruins' run to the Stanley Cup that a legend was born, that of "Sudden Death" Mel Hill. But, Hill's moment in history almost never happened and Roy Conacher played a significant role in the events surrounding the entire situation.

The date was April 2, 1939, the seventh and deciding game of the Stanley Cup semi-final series between the host Boston Bruins and the visiting New York Rangers had gone in to triple overtime. Hill, and the Rangers, "Muzz" Patrick were sent off for roughing. With the teams playing four aside, league scoring champion, Roy Conacher took a shot at the net. He beat the goalie, Bert Gardiner, but to the disappointment of the Bruins' faithful, there a resounding "clang" as Roy's shot deflected off the goal post. Shortly afterward, Conacher found himself with the puck and the Ranger goalie out of position. The league's top sniper, fired, and missed the net. As

Patrick and Hill returned to the ice Conacher once again led the Bruins' charge into the Rangers' end. The puck changed hands a few times before Bill Cowley fired a pass to Mel Hill, who in turn fired his shot and scored. Sending the Bruins to the finals against the Maple Leafs where they would capture the Stanley Cup. One has to wonder if Roy Conacher had notched the winning goal on either of his chances in that third overtime period, would he have forever been known as "Sudden Death".[144]

The Bruins continued to be a league power and two weeks later, on April 16, 1939, Roy Conacher, used his goal-scoring abilities to notch one of the biggest goals of his career. He bulged the twine with the game-winning and Cup-winning marker for the Bruins.

In fact, almost twenty years later, **Blueline Magazine**, asked Roy Conacher to write a story about the most impactful goal that he scored during his hockey career and also about his Cup-winning marker.

Conacher wrote that despite the fact that he had scored 26 goals in his rookie season, he had not been able to notch a marker in his hometown of Toronto. But in the fourth game of the finals, he broke this drought, scoring two goals to lead the Bruins to victory. Roy's decisive goal in that critical game in Maple Leaf Gardens occurred as the Leafs were attempting to mount a comeback. As the time clock ticked its way to the conclusion of the third period, and the end of the game, Toronto's desperation to record a win mounted. As Nick Metz attempted to start a rush out of the Leafs' end of the ice he attempted a pass that was deflected away from its target and came to rest a mere 25 feet in front of Turk Broda in the Leafs net.

> The crowd gasped when they saw that no Leaf was near the rubber, which had come to a full stop in the midst of wild action. Young Conacher streaked into action and grabbed the loose disc unhampered. He didn't fumble his chance. His wicked shot sagged the strings near the right goalpost before Broda could shift. And the verdict was in the bag for the Bruins.[145]

Then the teams headed back to Boston for what would be the fifth and final game of the playoffs where he would score what he called "the most thrilling goal I ever scored in hockey"[146].

In the fifth game, Conacher assisted on Mel Hill's first period goal. At the beginning of the third period, with the score notched at a one goal apiece, the pace of the game changed. This is how Roy Conacher remembered the events of that game:

> With elimination staring them in the face, Toronto really put on the pressure in that third period. We were scrambling around in our end of the rink when Eddie Shore passed the puck to me and, at the same time, Gordie Drillon made a move to check me. I dropped it over to Bill Cowley, then broke around Drillon, all this taking place behind our own

96

blue-line.

Then all heck broke loose. I raced up the ice, with Drillon right on my heels, and as I hit the Toronto defence, Cowley fed me the puck, which I trapped and scooted in on Turk Broda, the Toronto goal-tender. Broda took one look at the situation, then came out of his net quickly to smother any shot I might make. I just had time to shoot for the top right-hand corner, then went sprawling over Broda and along the ice into the corner of the rink. Frankly, I didn't know whether I had managed to pick the corner, then when I heard the screams and noises of the crowd, I knew I hadn't missed.[147]

That playoff was indeed a huge moment in Roy Conacher's hockey career. He was still a rookie, and he had led the league in goals during the regular season. But in the five-game final series against Toronto he notched 6 goals, two of them game-winners!

The Bruins' success during this stretch was helped significantly by a number of factors. Of course the famous "Kraut Line", along with a mix of veteran and youthful defenders were good reasons for Boston's successful run. But, the scoring prowess of "Three Gun Line" of Roy Conacher and his line mates, centreman Bill Cowley and right winger Eddie Wiseman, was considered by many to be a huge factor in the team's ongoing success.

But that run atop the NHL was about to come to an end. After Boston's second Stanley Cup victory in the 1940-41 NHL season, Roy's life changed dramatically. In September 1941 he married Frances Walker of Saskatoon, Saskatchewan. And, he enlisted in the Royal Canadian Air Force.

He spent his first three years in the RCAF, posted in Saskatchewan, and then he was sent to Dartmouth Nova Scotia on Canada's east coast. Although he had joined the Canadian war effort, Roy was able to continue playing hockey as he suited up for various RCAF amateur clubs that also featured other NHLers as his teammates.

After the Second World War concluded, Roy returned to the Bruins for the final games of the 1945-46 NHL hockey season and the playoffs. But his time in "Beantown" was about to come to an end.

The next season, 1946-47, saw him skating for the Detroit Red Wings. In the "Motor City" he experienced more offensive success, notching a career high 30 goals. Despite the fact that Roy's goal production was second only to Rocket Richard's league-leading 45 goals, his stay with the Wings would be abbreviated. The problems arose when he demanded a contract that would pay him $8,500 per season. Roy felt that this amount was commensurate with his offensive skills. However, Detroit felt that he should accept the same amount as his contract for the previous season, $6,500. Although the Red Wings later raised their offer to

$7,000, Roy still refused to play in the "Motor City" for anything less than the original amount he had requested and to emphasize his determination he returned to his home in Toronto.[148]

After the contract dispute lingered on, Detroit's irascible General Manager Jack Adams dealt Roy to New York for Ed Slowinski and a player to be named later. Adams probably dealt his high scoring forward more for vengeance than anything else because "Roy Conacher became the first regular season salary holdout"[149] to that date in the history of the Detroit franchise.

But, showing some of the stubbornness that had been illustrated more than a few times by his older brothers and would be further evidenced by future Conachers, Roy balked at this move and refused to report to New York and instead announced his intention to retire. He told the press:

> "I have plans for other things but I don't know just yet what I'll do." Asked for more definite retirement reasons, he replied: 'I've been thinking it over for a couple of years and became fed up with it.'
>
> To a question whether 'it' meant hockey generally, he laughed, then said, 'With people mostly.' He would not amplify.[150]

Undeterred in his quest to rid himself of Conacher, who had

dared to refuse to sign a contract, Adams then unloaded the "malcontent" to Chicago.[151] In that era of professional sports, players were considered mere chattels by their teams. It was expected that they would do as they were told. And, if they did not agree with their bosses they had two choices, shut up and follow orders, or get out of the game.[152]

It is interesting to note that the actual deal to get Roy Conacher into a Black Hawks' uniform was the result of a clandestine meeting between Bill Tobin, Chicago's President and management representatives from the Rangers which resulted in the Hawks paying New York $25,000 for Conacher's NHL rights.[153]

Roy spent four complete seasons with the Black Hawks. Each season he was amongst the top goal scorers and point leaders, not only on his team, but in the entire NHL. In the 1948-49 NHL season Roy captured the National Hockey League's scoring title. Despite his 26 goals and 42 assists, Conacher was unable to lift his team into the

Stanley Cup Playoffs. In fact, during his entire stay in the "Windy City", his team never made the playoffs. One has wonder how much greater his scoring totals might have been if he had played on stronger teams.

During the last few weeks of the scoring race, Conacher and his line mate, Doug Bentley, were battling for the title as the league's top sniper. They drew the ire of league president Clarence Campbell when the two Hawks announced that they would split the prize money which was $1,000 for the winner and $500 for the runner-up. "Campbell said the league would not recognize any such agreement."[154] Whether the two actually split their winnings is unknown.

Near the end of the next season, 1949-50, the question of retirement once again came to forefront of conversation between the media and Roy Conacher. Prior to a game on March 22, 1950 he told the press "that he was quitting professional hockey for good and would into business with his brothers"[155].

Of note, the hat trick that Roy netted that night against the Bruins was only the second hat trick recorded in the NHL that season. Gordie Howe was the other sniper to bag a trio of goals in one game.

Contrary to the retirement stories at the end of the season, Roy returned to Chicago for the 1950-51 NHL campaign. He had not lost his scoring touch as he recorded 26 goals and 24 assists with lowly Black Hawks. But in February 1951 an event occurred that surprised everyone who knew Roy Conacher.

It happened in a game with the Maple Leafs. At 17:27 of the third period with the Hawks down a goal and pressing to get the tying marker, referee Hugh McLean sent Chicago's Jim Conacher (who was not a relation to Roy) to the penalty box. The entire Hawks team was incensed at the call, because it probably meant an end to their comeback to tie the game.

At the penalty box, the referee was surrounded by angry Chicago players when Roy Conacher rushed towards the penalty box. He "dropped his gloves on the way, as if he meant to fight, and when he made his way through the mob and pushed McLean hard."[156]

The amazement about how Roy had acted out of character was echoed by the league's president in his statement about the incident and his defence of the referee's action. Clarence Campbell said that he was "perturbed to learn that Roy Conacher, one of the quietest and most gentlemanly players in the league, had apparently attempted to molest an official."[157]

After he played 12 games in the 1951-52 campaign, Roy retired from NHL play. Some say that family rivalries kept Roy playing in the NHL until he had notched his 226 sixth career goal. Why 226 goals you may ask? The answer is simple this number represents one more goal than his brother Charlie had netted during his NHL career. Brian Conacher described this rivalry between his two uncles, Roy and Charlie, as, Roy saying, "...he wanted to score one more goal than Uncle Charlie, so he wouldn't have to listen to him 'yak' for the rest of his life."[158]

After retiring from NHL action, Roy Conacher did not turn his back on the game of hockey for the next decade or more when he joined with his brothers playing in numerous charity hockey games and he participated as an instructor at various hockey schools.

Like his brothers he was a multi-sport athlete of some repute. Roy and his brothers also participated in many charity softball games. In 1955, he accepted the position of assistant manager and golf pro at the Wasaga Golf and Country Club.

Toronto Star columnist, Jim Proudfoot, made an interesting note in a column about Roy Conacher's scoring prowess, at the time of the youngest Conacher's induction to the Hockey Hall of Fame. Proudfoot, himself a Hall of Famer, illustrated that if Conacher had remained in the NHL rather than joining the armed forces in the Second World War, his legacy as a dynamic goal scorer might have been entirely different. Proudfoot wrote, that if "you could imagine a modest 25 (goals) each of those four wartime campaigns he missed, he'd have gone out as the biggest shooter in NHL history up till then."[159]

NOTE: Roy Conacher is the uncle of Murray Armstrong, a centre, who enjoyed an NHL career with the Toronto Maple Leafs, New York Americans, and the Detroit Red Wings. He played 270 games in the big leagues scoring 67 goals and 121 assists. He was teammate of Charlie Conacher, for a time, in both Toronto and with the New York Americans.

Chapter Five

Pete Conacher

Charles William "Pete" Conacher Jr. made his debut into the world on July 29, 1932. His early years were spent in the St. Clair Avenue and Arlington Avenue area which is about equidistant between Bathurst and Dufferin Streets in the City of Toronto's north end. He attended McMurrich Public School until Grade Two when he, and his mother "Bobby"[160], moved to Millwood Road in the Leaside area of east Toronto and Pete enrolled in Bessborough Public School.

It was in Leaside that Pete became an eager participant in the world of sports. He recalls skating on an outdoor rink at Millwood Park playing hockey. When he became eligible to play in an organized hockey league, he suited up for the Bessborough Pee Wee team. The next step in his young hockey career was skating with the North Toronto Kinsmen Terrriers bantam team. The following season he joined the Leaside Lions bantam club.

He attended Leaside High School and as a teenager he played softball for a team from St. Cuthbert's Anglican Church.

As a teenager he continued his hockey career, when as Pete remembers, Chris Walroth of the Lions organization put together a

Minor Midget hockey team known as the Williams Tobacco club. The new club achieved immediate success, capturing the Toronto Hockey League Minor Midget title.

The next season, the club moved into the Midget ranks of the Toronto Hockey League. Once again, they were a dominant force in the league. However, their march to the THL Midget title ended when they were eliminated in the Championship final round.

After playing minor hockey it is the hope of most youngsters that the next step will be a call to play junior hockey. Pete recalls how he ended up playing OHA Junior "A" hockey with the Galt Black Hawks. Although he was known as a talented player, there had been no "hype" about where he was going to extend his hockey career. The son of Toronto hockey legend Charlie Conacher read in the newspaper that he was going to be given a tryout with the Galt team. Until the moment he read about his tryout, he had not had any indication that an OHA Junior "A" club was interested in him.[161]

Before he suited up with Galt, and after he turned 16 years old, Pete signed a "D" form with the Chicago Black Hawks, which permitted him to play in Galt and gave his hockey rights to the NHL club.

Growing up in Toronto, the shadow of his father Charlie "The Big Bomber" Conacher, must have loomed large over his road hockey games and minor hockey experiences. Pete never really felt a lot of pressure from others,

I guess I probably felt a little bit of pressure. My dad, being Charlie, and then Lionel and Roy, but I never felt pressure from my teammates or management. I never felt pressure from them. I think if I felt pressure, it was just because I put it on myself. And more pressure from fans than teammates or management.[162]

His hockey skills became more noticeable as he progressed through the ranks of the Toronto Hockey League, especially when teams that he skated for claimed THL titles twice in a three-year span from 1947 to 1949.

When asked about who his childhood hockey heroes were, Pete is quick to respond. The first player named might come as a surprise to many. It was Kenny Smith[163], a left winger with the Oshawa Generals of the OHA Junior "A" loop. Conacher explained how Smith became his hero by saying that when his father was coaching the Generals, he would sometimes get to attend the games. And he says that it was not hard to spot Smith's talents as he played on a line with future NHL star Floyd Curry and centreman "Red" Tilson[164].

But, it is safe to say, that the biggest influence on Pete Conacher was his uncle, Roy Conacher. Pete says that his uncle played "my style of hockey, he didn't look for trouble and instead relied on his skating and other hockey skills."[165]These were very good reasons to style his game after his uncle.

Pete has fond memories of his uncles Roy and Bert, and his cousin Murray Henderson, who he says were "like big brothers to me". And he has fond memories of his grandparents, "who he says were very close to me."[166]

Ironically, two of Pete's hockey heroes, his Uncle Roy and Cousin Murray, would spend a brief time[167] as teammates with the Boston Bruins.

Pete's hockey career began in earnest when he left his family home in Toronto and headed to Galt for a three-year stint in the OHA junior league. If there were any questions that the young Conacher was a talent in his own right they were quickly dispersed by the end of his first junior season. He was a goal scorer there was no doubt!

In his rookie season, Pete potted 24 goals in 45 games and added 26 assists for a better than a point a game average. In his second season, he continued his scoring touch, notching 32 goals and 32 assists in 52 games. And, perhaps to further the mystique of his superstar father, the Galt Black Hawks issued him a jersey with his father's number 9 on the back.

The number "9" on his jersey had more profound implications for Pete than simply because it was his father's jersey number. Today, Pete's home boasts a picture on a wall of his uncle Roy presenting him with a "9" Black Hawks' jersey. Because that was also Roy Conacher's jersey number when he played, not only for the Black Hawks, for most of his NHL career! Of particular interest is that when Roy Conacher played in Detroit in 1946-47 season, he wore number 9 on his Red Wings jersey and Gordie Howe, the man who would make the number famous in the "Motor City" wore "17"!

During his second season in Galt, he was partnered on his forward line with Ken Wharram, who would become an NHL star. Although they clicked almost immediately as an effective offensive threat, it would be the following season, 1951-52, that the two youngsters would really make names for themselves as potent goal scorers.

Today, Pete recalls that Wharram is one of the best players that he ever played with. Wharram was centreman at that time and because Ken was a right hand shot, it was natural for him to pass to his left winger. Conacher says "I fitted Kenny and Kenny fitted me."[168]

Ironically, Wharram and Conacher would once again lineup as teammates playing with the Buffalo Bisons in the American Hockey League. Their paths would cross from time-to-time during the 1955-56, 1956-57, and 1957-58 AHL seasons.

Perhaps it was the new number "9" on his jersey, or it was simply a case of building confidence, but in his last season of junior hockey, Pete fired home an incredible, for that era, 53 goals in only 51 games. Proving that he was more than a shooter, young Conacher also recorded 67 assists.[169] His 120 scoring points helped him win the Belmore Trophy as Most Valuable Player.

His stats for that final season in Galt were so impressive that he gained the attention of the parent NHL club. Pete received the call that every young hockey player dreams of getting. He was summoned to play in the NHL! His two-game stint during the 1951-52 season probably had many people thinking that this was the beginning of a career with the NHL's Chicago Black Hawks.

Conacher's call up was trumpeted by the Chicago media and the club's top brass. In a story announcing the arrival of the son of a former coach and the nephew of a former Hawk scoring star, a sports writer said that Pete is "rated as a speedy skater and a top shotmaker"[170]. Club president Bill Tobin was even more exuberant saying of Pete's arrival, "Conacher is the start of a youth movement" and that he came "from a great family of hockey stars."[171]

Pete's first NHL training camp in September 1952 had sports writers, and probably the Black Hawks management, ecstatic about the arrival of another Conacher in the NHL. An article about Pete's scoring feats in a recent pair of exhibition games between the Hawks and the Stanley Cup Champion Detroit Red Wings said:

> Pete Conacher, youngest active member of one of hockey's oldest and most celebrated families, is one of the standouts in the Chicago Black Hawks training camp.

The 20-year-old Conacher, son of the famed Charlie

Conacher and nephew of both Lionel and Roy Conacher, has scored three goals against Terry Sawchuk during exhibition games between Detroit and Chicago.[172]

This inspired story about the young rookie scoring three goals was probably enhanced due to the fact that on all three goals, he had beaten the goalie, who was considered by many to be the best netminder in the NHL. After all, the previous playoff season, Sawchuk had recorded four shutouts as the Red Wings swept their way to the Stanley Cup Championship winning an incredible eight straight games.[173]

Pete's professional hockey career began in the 1952-53 hockey season when he played for the St. Louis Flyers of the American Hockey League and the Chicago Black Hawks. On October 31, 1952 the media was once again extolling the scoring virtues of the young Conacher. In an article entitled, "Pete Conacher Shines", the story is all about Pete scoring two goals and one assist as he led the Hawks to victory over the New York Rangers.[174]

The next season, 1953-54, found Pete skating on a regular basis with the Black Hawks. His goal-scoring histrionics in junior had his NHL coaches and managers hoping for similar results in the big leagues. Perhaps his greatest night occurred on March 19, 1954. That night he scored the Hawks' first hat trick of the season as Chicago dumped the Bruins 7-0.[175] His 19-goal total in his rookie season must has been a cause for hope for future greatness from the kid with the famous last name.

If a "sophomore jinx" is a possibility, then Pete Conacher would definitely be a believer. In an era when a 20-goal season was considered outstanding in the NHL, a 19-goal rookie campaign was certainly cause for hope on the part of both Conacher and his bosses in Chicago. However, a repeat of his rookie season scoring magic was not to be.

After recording only 2 goals and 4 assists in 18 games, the Black Hawks traded Pete to the New York Rangers in a multi-player deal. He, and future Hall of Fame defenceman Bill Gadsby, went to the Rangers for Rich Lamoureux, Nick Mickoski and another future Hall of Fame defenceman, Allan Stanley on November 23, 1954.

He spent the rest of the 1954-55 season and the first part of the 1955-56 season skating on Broadway. His scoring numbers were reasonable, scoring 11 goals and adding 11 assists in 41 games. But despite the fact that his production numbers were better than the previous season when he had recorded 12 goals and 11 assists in 70 games when he suited up for both the Hawks and the Rangers, it was not enough to keep him in the NHL. He was demoted to the American Hockey League's Buffalo Bisons.

On June 4, 1957, Pete became a member of the Toronto Maple Leafs when he was drafted from the New York Rangers' organization. This was probably the fulfilment of a childhood dream for a youngster who had grown up in Toronto cheering for the hometown team. And, when you add to the equation the fact that his father was one of the biggest stars in the history of the Maple Leafs' franchise, this must have been a welcome opportunity after the failed promise of his NHL experiences in Chicago and New York.

His arrival in Toronto came as complete surprise to Conacher. He told a reporter that

> He hadn't expected to be drafted by any National Hockey League club this season, let alone the Maple Leafs. Not after what he calls 'the bad year' he had with Buffalo Bisons last winter.
>
> "Surprised? I thought they were kidding when they told me", grinned Conacher last night. "I thought I had such a poor season with the Bisons that they'd pass me up."…"I'm glad to get another chance at the big time.[176]

In retrospect, Pete now suspects that Billy Reay was the reason that the Leafs drafted him. Reay had just been appointed the Leafs' coach. The previous season Reay had coached Toronto's AHL farm club in Rochester and Conacher considers that the new coach had seen him play often in Buffalo and this may have precipitated his acquisition in the draft.

Like his father, and his uncles, Pete was a multi-sport athlete. Conacher played baseball with the 'Lizzies' of the Playground Senior Baseball League two nights a week. And, he suited up three nights a week with the 'Latimers' of the Beaches Major League softball loop.[177]

When asked about his son playing hockey in Toronto, Charlie Conacher enthused, "I'm pleased Pete is joining the Leafs. I think he's a lot better than he has shown, and it's a good opportunity for him."[178]

But, Pete recalls that playing in Toronto was not all that he expected.

> That was an entirely different feeling putting on the Leaf uniform because I was from Toronto and because my dad had played in Toronto and had made his reputation in Toronto. So that was a little different. I felt a lot of pressure.[179]

Unfortunately, Conacher never really got a chance to perform in Toronto. Prior to the season's start he tore some ligaments in his knee and missed the first few weeks of the season. Then when he returned, he was injured again. Pete recalls that it happened when Bob Bailey "popped me into the boards, injuring my chest" and "I was out for another couple of weeks."[180]

When he finally returned to game action, Pete played five games in the blue and white jersey of his hometown team recording only one assist. He remembers that he did score one goal for the Leafs. It happened in a game against Detroit. With the score notched at 3-3, and clock ticking down, Pete fired a shot at the net and it went in. Unfortunately, the time clock registered 20:00 and the horn went to signal the end of the game just as the puck bulged the twine. Because the blue light went on before the goal light, the goal was nullified.

After his fifth game with Toronto, he was demoted to the team's farm club in Rochester. Pete requested, and was granted a trade to his old AHL team in Buffalo instead. He would never play in the NHL again.

At the end of the 1957-58 hockey season, Pete made a dramatic career decision. He applied for amateur status and joined the Belleville McFarlands in time to suit up for the World Hockey Championships.

And, in what he called "a thrill for me"[181] he was a key component in Belleville's march to capturing the World Championship for Canada in the tournament held in Prague Czechoslovakia. In the 8-game series, Pete scored 7 goals and added three assists.

Pete's hockey career did not end with his gold-medal winning performance with the Belleville McFarlands. The following season he returned to the ranks of professional hockey with his former club, the Buffalo Bisons, for the 1959-60 AHL season. In Buffalo he recorded only 5 goals and 10 assists. But it was the next season, 1960-61, that would see Conacher once again become a potent offensive threat.

The revival of his scoring magic coincided with his move to another American Hockey League club, the Hershey Bears. His first season in Hershey he more than doubled his output from the previous year banging home 11 goals and recording 24 assists. But things were only going to get better!

For the next four seasons Pete's scoring totals would place him in the upper echelons of the AHL's scoring statistics[182]. Conacher had notched his third hat trick of the season against Rochester.[183] Interestingly two of the defenders he beat to score the three goals are now honoured members of the Hockey Hall of Fame, goalie Gerry Cheevers and defenceman Al Arbour!

Pete credits his success with Hershey as partly due to a shift in positions and the opportunity to play with another great centreman. For some reason the coach moved Conacher to right wing on a line centred by Mike Nykoluk. Pete said that once that move had been made "I had some good years, mostly because of Mike"[184] centring my line.

But in his sixth season in Hershey his point production dropped significantly. His goal totals fell to 14 and he garnered only 20 assists. At the end of the 1965 -66 hockey season he retired from the game that he loved so much.

But like his generation of Conachers and those of his father's, Pete was well-prepared for life after hockey. In an era when hockey players needed another job to supplement their hockey income, Pete had made some wise moves. He had taken off-season employment with companies on the Toronto Stock Exchange. So, when he retired from professional hockey it was only natural that he would become a full-time stock trader, a profession that he would enjoy until he retired in 1995.

Pete Conacher is "very proud of the family and the family name and what they accomplished in hockey"[185]. But, given his statistics and successes, one can see that he made it in the world of hockey because of talent, especially his ability to score goals. In 2010, Pete's contributions and successes during his hockey career were recognized when he was inducted as an honoured member into the Bobby Orr Hall of Fame in Parry Sound Ontario.

Chapter Six

<u>Brian Conacher</u>

"When you bear the name of your game's royal family, individual identity is impossible, achievement more difficult and comparison unavoidable and constant. For Brian Conacher, that comparison should be staggering – son of Lionel and nephew of Charlie and Roy."[186]

These were the words penned by **Toronto Star** sports writer Ken McKee on the occasion of relating the details of Brian Conacher's first game as a Toronto Maple Leaf.

Brian Conacher, born August 31, 1941, is the youngest of Lionel Conacher's five children. Brian says that his father and his uncles "...had successfully used sports as a springboard to a different kind of life from that into which they had been born".[187] Further to this point, Brian suggests: "My father died when I was twelve years old. If he had lived, I think I would probably never have played professional hockey."[188]

I knew my father was someone special because of his athletic achievements, but to me he was just my dad who was a federal Member of Parliament. I never knew him as an athlete. I played many sports as I grew up, and I loved them all. My dad encouraged me to participate, but never pushed. Both my mother and father were adamant that all five children (I'm the youngest) get an education, and we were pushed to academics more than athletics when we were young; we were expected to go to university, and sports were always second.[189]

When approached about his hockey career, Brian is quite candid about his abilities and his hockey legacy. "By his own admission, Brian Conacher became more famous because of his surname than for his own exploits as a professional hockey player, 'I was a journeyman player who had a modest, inconspicuous career'."[190]

Because of their father's successes, the need to play sports solely for the purpose of improving their economic and social status was never an issue for Brian and his siblings. Lionel had retired from the sporting life before Brian was born. But one would assume that there would be discussion around the family home about the father's exploits. However, this does seem to have been the situation as Lionel's athletic endeavours were never really talked about around the house. Brian says "I think I have learned more about my father's career in sports from other people than I ever did at home."[191] Continuing in that stream of thought the youngest Conacher says that "...in the twelve years I knew my father, there was never any push in the direction of playing any sports and certainly nothing in particular about hockey."[192]

As a youngster, Brian was limited to playing hockey on outdoor skating rinks participating mostly in pickup games and neighbourhood scrimmages. His parents refused overtures from organized hockey teams that wished to sign their youngest son to play for them. It seems that his parents wanted him to enjoy sports and not be caught up in the competitive atmosphere that so often surrounds hockey leagues in Canada, even at the youngest of ages. It was not until he was a teenager that Brian was able to suit up with a team.

Ironically, Brian's parents, or his father at least, had made this decision for Brian long before he was born.[193]

Writing in 1970, Brian described his perspective on how his father came to some of his decisions with regards to what he wanted for his children:

> It was while he (Lionel) was living his athletic career that his mind was becoming set that his children would not have to do the same. With an education, sport would always be a choice, rather than necessity. My father had struggled so he, too, had that choice. Looking back, I can see that we were surrounded, quite deliberately, with opportunities leading to a way of life in which one makes one's living more with the brain than with the body.[194]

Lionel Conacher and his siblings had grown up in near poverty conditions. Consequently a significant goal for them was better opportunities for their children. Lionel's success in achieving this goal was perhaps evident from the fact that he was able to send his sons to one of the most prestigious private schools in the country, Upper Canada College, while his daughters attended the equally esteemed Havergal College.

It was while he was attending Upper Canada College that Brian finally was allowed to play for a formal hockey team. At age 14, he played not only hockey for Upper Canada College, but he also suited up for the school's football team. But the pressures of organized hockey would soon surface in his teenage life.

At age 17, "I was confronted not with an offer to play organized hockey, but an ultimatum."[195] The threat came from the Toronto Maple Leafs organization. They told Brian that if he did not accept their offer sheet and play junior hockey with the Marlies, then he could be vulnerable to being drafted by a junior club located elsewhere in Ontario. To avoid this possibility, the Conacher family agreed to Brian signing a contract which paid his school tuition and provided him with $60 a week.[196] His mother also insisted that playing for the Marlies must not interfere with his schooling.[197]

Like his father and his two older brothers, Brian was an outstanding football player. He played the sport in high school and at university. In fact, his prowess on the gridiron was recognized in

122

1962 when he was named an intercollegiate all-star halfback with the University of Western Ontario.

The Leafs organization played hard ball to get Lionel's youngest son to sign a contract. But their motives could be summed up simply by a statement made by Toronto's vice-president, Harold Ballard, "Sure we want him for his name. With that name, he has to be a good one."[198] One has to wonder if Ballard was referring to Conacher as a good hockey player or a good box office attraction.

The threat of being forced to played somewhere outside of the Toronto area was very real. There were rumours that the Detroit Red Wings were interested in acquiring his rights. It may not necessarily have been his hockey skills that was the reason why the Red Wings were considering him. Brian wrote that his "Aunt Queen lived in Detroit and knew lots of the hockey crowd, and she said they were interested in anyone named Conacher."[199]

After a career in junior hockey, Brian was not about to take the step to professional hockey without thought and consideration to what his options were. Perhaps it was his parents' influence growing up that caused him to explore his options or possibly it was about something his mother told him. Brian said that when he was deciding which path to follow after junior hockey, his mother told him that his father had ignored an opportunity to play for Canada's hockey team in the 1924 Olympics and that he had regretted that decision for the rest of his life.

Whatever, the reason, he joined Father David Bauer's Canadian hockey program. This would offer him the opportunity to try out for the 1964 Canadian Olympic hockey team, and perhaps fulfill his father's missed opportunity. But Brian did not devote all of his time to hockey, he also enrolled at the University of Western Ontario.

At the 1964 Olympics, Conacher was introduced to the world of international amateur hockey. It was in Innsbruck Austria the he learned about true might and skill of the Russian hockey program. And, he also learned a lot about the politics of international hockey. In a radio interview Brian said that during the third period of Canada's game against the Russians, a group of officials got together and changed the tie-breaking criteria for hockey medals. The result of this action dropped the Canadian Olympic hockey team to fourth place in the final standings.[200]

The Canadians finished out of the medals. Many of the players and other members of the Canadian national hockey program were quite vocal about the abilities of the Russians and many of the other European hockey programs. Unfortunately, their opinions fell upon the deaf ears of the NHL and North American hockey fans in general. One has to wonder if these warnings from the 1964 Canadian Olympians had been heeded, the circumstances around the drama of the 1972 Canada-Russia Super Series might have been much different!

Lionel and Brian both shared the opinion that international sports needed to open its doors to athletes whether they were amateur or professional. Brian suggested that the use of professionals at the Olympics had "taken away some of the hypocrisy"[201]. Many years earlier, when Lionel was asked for a solution to how Canada should select its 1948 Olympic team, he did not pull any punches, saying that he would

> "...select the best athletes in assorted forms of sport and send them to the games regardless of actual or suspected status as takers of ye nourishing greenback. Instead of the stereotyped formula, 'is he, or she, an amateur?' the only question Conacher's Olympic committee would ask is: 'is he, or she, good enough in quality to carry the athletic torch for Canada'.[202]

Without is father to provide guidance when the time came to turn pro as a hockey player Brian turned to his uncle Charlie for advice.[203]

Brian held out as a rookie with the Leafs organization trying to get some assurances that he would play in Toronto rather than any of their minor professional teams[204]. He told a reporter that if he did not sign with the Leafs, he could always attend the University of Western Ontario in London. Continuing that thought process he said that he didn't think that he had to stick around training camp "for a month and play 20 exhibition games" to prove that he belonged in the NHL. After all, he said "I don't want to miss too much school if that's where I am going to wind up."[205] But, Leaf management was not about to allow a rookie, even if his name was Conacher, dictate where he played.

Brian did not make the direct jump from amateur hockey to the NHL. Instead, he spent his first full season in professional hockey, 1965-66, with the Maple Leafs' top farm club, the Rochester Americans. He notched 14 goals and 16 assists in the American Hockey League. These were not numbers that would ordinarily get you promoted to the NHL, but it was more likely his skills as a defensive forward and his hard-working style of play that probably induced Punch Imlach, Toronto's Coach and General Manager, to make a place for Brian on the Leafs' roster for the 1966-67 NHL season.

On October 22, 1966, Brian made his NHL debut against the New York Rangers. After a mere 58 seconds Conacher notched his first goal and later in the second period he netted another to help the Leafs to 4-4 tie. There was a certain irony about his goal-scoring exploits. It was reported that at a family reunion, of sorts, the night before the game, Brian had heard someone relate that "your Uncle Charlie scored in his first game. Wouldn't it be nice…?"[206] Well, it was nice and Brian one-upped his famous uncle by scoring not once, but twice in his Maple Leafs' debut!

Conacher produced a respectable 14 goals and 13 assists that season and once again demonstrated a great work ethic and paid strict attention to his defensive play. One of the goals that he notched in his rookie season was a game-winning tally to give the Leaf a 3-2 victory over the Montreal Canadiens on November 30, 1966. This marker prompted Conn Smythe to heap some high praise on the youngster saying: "That Conacher is much like his father (Lionel) and his uncle (Charlie) when they broke into the NHL."[207]

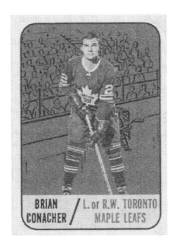

Brian's play during the season caught the attention of many of the voters charged with selecting the league's rookie of the year. But there was probably never any doubt as to who would capture NHL's Rookie of the Year trophy that season. After all, Conacher's rookie season, was also the rookie season of a defenseman playing for the Boston Bruins by the name of Bobby Orr.

Describing his method of playing hockey, Brian told Stan

Obodiac,

> I don't approach hockey differently from anything else. I go
> about school and hockey the same way. If you stick at it and
> work at with an honest effort, over the long haul it is going to
> work out all right.[208]

Brian's rookie season was not completed with the final
whistle of the last game of the regular season. The Leafs made the
Stanley Cup play-offs. In post-season play, Conacher was a force at
both ends of the ice. Not only did he record 3 goals and 2 assists, but
his stellar defensive work checking the opposition's top offensive
threats was equally important to Toronto's drive to capture the
Stanley Cup.

Two of Conacher's playoff markers came on Tuesday April
18, 1967, helping Toronto eliminate the Chicago Black Hawks from
the playoffs in the sixth game of the semi-final round. About his
Game 6 heroics, Brian recalls, "I still can't believe I got two playoff
goals in one game."[209]

Despite all of the pressure of Stanley Cup playoff action,
Brian and the rest of the Conacher clan must have been on an
emotional roller-coaster that day in April as Brian's uncle, Charlie
had undergone surgery for throat cancer.

Charlie Conacher, had been a member of the Toronto Maple
Leafs' first Stanley Cup winning team and in the spring of 1967, his

128

nephew, Brian Conacher, would be a member of Toronto's most recent Stanley Cup winning team.

After the festivities surrounding the team's Stanley Cup victory, in May of the same year, Brian started a new round of celebrations. With his Uncle Charlie, in attendance, Brian got married. The various magazines and newspapers played up the wedding as evidence of the youngest Conacher's social standing. **The Hockey Pictorial** described events surrounding the nuptials saying that Brian "…is considered a social lion in some quarters" elaborating further that

> Last May he was married at Upper Canada College and the wedding reception was at the Granite Club. He honeymooned in the Bahamas and returned to a round of social lionizing including a wine and cheese party, a sherry party, a cocktail party and a swimming party.[210]

The following season, 1967-68, did not start out on a positive vein. Brian found himself locked in a contract dispute with the Maple Leafs. When the dust settled, Brian had signed a two-year contract for a reported $20,000 a year. Conacher netted 11 goals and 14 assists with the Leafs, but once again found himself in the AHL, skating for 5 games with Rochester.

At the Intra-League Draft in June 1968, Brian's NHL rights were acquired by the Detroit Red Wings. Perhaps it was his sense of not wanting to be controlled by professional hockey as to where he

129

could, and could not play, that led Conacher to leave the ranks of professional hockey and return to the Canadian National Team.

One has to wonder if Brian's demotion to Rochester and the fact that the Maple Leafs left his rights exposed in the 1968 Intra-League Draft were a result of his extended hold-out for a better contract at the beginning of the season or whether it was due to an action that Brian took that year. He joined the National Hockey League Players Association.[211]

Today, every NHL player is a member of the NHLPA, but at that time players were under a lot of pressure from the management of their teams not to enlist with the players' union. For Brian, and many other hockey players, the idea of joining a union was not something that they probably had ever considered during their journey to the NHL. Conacher recalled: "I didn't grow up in a union work culture; my attitude was, if there was a job to do you did what was needed to get it done on a timely basis."[212]

He remained with the Canadian hockey program for the next three seasons. But during that time what he disliked the most about being a chattel controlled by professional hockey was clearly exhibited. While he was absent from the professional game his rights were traded from Detroit to Minnesota[213]. Then, about a year later his rights were once again on the move, this time back to Toronto[214]. In August 1970, his rights were dealt back to Detroit[215]. Ironically, during this whole process Brian was happily playing amateur hockey for the Canada's National Team!

He made an attempt to return to the NHL for the 1971-72 hockey season. Conacher played with Fort Worth of the Central Hockey League scoring 13 goals and adding 13 assists in 40 regular season games and he registered an additional three goals and two assists in seven playoff games. That season he also skated for 22 games with the Detroit Red Wings notching three goals and one assist.

It was after he left the "Motor City" that Brian had his name etched into the NHL Record books for a unique situation. According the Brian's biographical sketch on the SIHR[216] website, he was the last National Hockey League player to wear glasses during game action. He stopped wearing glasses at the end of the 1971-72 NHL season.

In September 1972, Brian's journey in the world of hockey

took another turn. He was hired to work as the colour commentator, alongside broadcasting legend Foster Hewitt, for the 1972 Canada-Russia Super Series. One of the major reasons that Conacher landed this highly sought-after job was his many years of playing international hockey against the Russians and other European teams while he was a member of the Canadian National Hockey program. His familiarity with both the international game and his experience as an NHL player positioned him above other possible competitors for this job.

This would not be his first job broadcasting international hockey games. In 1969, Johnny Esaw of CTV Sports had hired Brian to provide colour commentary for the World Hockey Championships in Sweden.

Conacher's involvement in the 1972 Super Series followed a rather tenuous path. At first he was hired for the job and then Brian was abruptly fired. In his memoirs, **As the Puck Turns: A Personal Journey Through the World of Hockey**, Conacher provides a very thought-provoking idea as to why he was summarily removed from this broadcasting position. He wrote:

> Why had the NHL objected to my involvement? Since I
> wrote **Hockey in Canada: The Way It Is!** (1970) I had been
> persona non grata with the NHL. My criticism of the way the
> league controlled and manipulated the game and its players,
> and league's continual undermining of the efforts and success

132

of the Nats program as envisioned by Father Bauer, irked the NHL bosses big time. The NHL wanted nothing happening in hockey in Canada, and in particular the NHL, which they didn't control. And they definitely didn't control me.[217]

How Brian regained his position in the broadcast booth with Foster Hewitt was partially due to his father in some sort of manner. It seems that Father Athol Murray of the Notre Dame School in Wilcox, Saskatchewan was upset by the decision to oust Conacher from the broadcasting team. So he took his objections to John Bassett Sr., the owner of CTV.

Brian suggests that one of the reasons Father Murray took exception the NHL's action was that "He was a great admirer of my father, Lionel, and appreciated my involvement in the formative years of the Nats program."[218] As quickly as he had been fired, Conacher was reinstated to work on the broadcast of this historic series.

Brian's work in the 1972 Super Series would lead to an assignment with ABC Sports when that American-based television network provided coverage of the 1976 Winter Olympics. Working on the 1972 Canada-Russia series gave Conacher the opportunity to work with a Canadian and hockey broadcasting icon, Foster Hewitt. At the Innsbruck games he had the good fortune to work with a legendary American sportscasting icon, Curt Gowdy. In 1988 he would once again go behind the microphone to deliver the colour commentary for hockey games at the 1988 Winter Olympics in Calgary with CBC Radio.

After the 1972 Super Series came to a conclusion, Conacher decided to give professional hockey another try. His team, and league, of choice was the Ottawa Nationals of the newly-formed World Hockey Association. Once again, Brian's decision to move to the WHA seems to have been his way of demonstrating his desire to choose his own hockey destination instead of allowing his rights to controlled by others, namely NHL teams.

After playing in 69 regular season games and scoring eight goals and 19 assists along with one goal and three assists in 5 playoff games, Brian retired once again as an active player and looked for further opportunities in the world of hockey such as a coaching position.[219]

Perhaps illustrating this possibility is a comment made to Brian by John Bassett Jr., after he purchased the Toronto Toros of the WHA. Conacher asked Bassett about a coaching job with the Toros. He told Brian that he was going to keep the team's coaching staff. And, perhaps because he felt that Brian was a bit too idealistic he commented: "You've a great sense of the way things should be, but not a great sense of the way they are."[220]

Undeterred, Conacher let it be known to many people that he was interested in a coaching position. With some help from Buck Houle, the Toros general manager, in 1973, he landed the dual

134

portfolio of coach and general manager of the Mohawk Valley Comets (formerly the Clinton Comets of the now-defunct EHL) of the NAHL. Brian would remain with the club until 1976.

His first off-ice job in hockey would prove to be a training ground for his future endeavours. His responsibilities with the Comets went far beyond player personnel and on-ice performance, Brian had to handle all of the team's financial responsibilities including fund-raising. The job was a tall-order for a rookie coach and general manager, especially when one considers that the Comets were a basement-dwelling hockey team.

Besides the duties of general manager, Brian had to coach the team. He had never coached before, but Conacher decided to model his coaching after Father David Bauer, who Brian said, was "the best coach I ever had"[221].

The 1974-75 season saw some better results for the team. Despite a losing season, 31 wins and 38 losses, the team made the playoffs and Brian was named the NAHL GM of the Year.

As he was always on the lookout to expand the player pool that would be available to him to improve the Comets, Brian developed a relationship with the Indianapolis Racers of the WHA and he created an agreement with the Buffalo Sabres to expand the source of players that he might be able to get for his team. Ironically, Brian's first general manager, Punch Imlach, and his first pro coach, Joe Crozier, held those same positions with the Sabres. Consequently, he

135

wondered what kind of a reception he would receive when he met them for the first time holding the same positions that they did.

My last contact with Punch had been when he unceremoniously dumped me from the Leafs in 1968. I didn't know what to expect when I showed up at his training camp. Some seven years older with real hockey management experience under my belt, I better appreciated some of the decisions Punch made over the years now that I, too, was trying to build a team and remain competitive and financially viable both on and off the ice. To my surprise, we got along very well, and he made a real effort to help the Comets. It was an interesting evolution of our relationship.[222]

In order to stay under the league budget limits, Brian was forced to suit up for three games when a number of his regular players were injured at the same time and unable to play. Conacher notched 2 goals and 1 assist in that troika of hockey contests.

In the mid-1970s, Conacher was approached by a group interested in shooting a movie about hockey and they wanted to rent the team's bus. The movie would be called "Slapshot" and it would feature Hollywood superstar Paul Newman in the leading role. Most of the actual hockey players to be used in the film would be players from the NAHL. Even the Comets' general manager would have role in the movie.

However Brian's role would be short-lived. "I played a referee and patrolled the ice on the side away from where the cameras were shooting the incident in the stands. Consequently, I ended up on the cutting room floor."[223]

Little did Brian realize it but his time with the Comets was to come to an end. Early in the 1976-77 hockey season, he was approached about taking the position of general manager of Indianapolis Racers of the WHA. Before accepting an offer, which was in reality a promotion of sorts, he did a lot of soul-searching.

I asked myself why I wanted to get into another financial struggle, only with a couple of more zeroes added on. But the WHA was the major leagues and where the opportunity was. So the options had been pretty clear: either take the job and be a part of major-league hockey, or pass and stay buried in the minor leagues, possibly forever.[224]

After he accepted the position he made a very disturbing discovery. "The serious financial challenges of the Racers made those of the Comets seem miniscule. I felt as if I had jumped out of the frying pan into fire, and a very hot one at that."[225]

After his examination of the financial records, Brian realized that there was not enough money to sustain the team. The ownership group had been convinced to contribute another $600,000 to the running of the team, but Conacher's research showed that even this amount would not be enough to run the club.

The previous management had not given him (the primary owner Harold Ducote) all the information, particularly information about some of the player contracts. The Racers probably should have folded before the owners hired me.[226]

When it looked like the Racers were about to fold, key members of the ownership group encouraged Brian to seek an opportunity for himself elsewhere in the league. To further this possibility, the team sent Conacher to the league meetings, not only to represent the Racers, but also to help him scout out a potential job. Brian sought to meet Nelson Skalbania, who, with Peter Polklington, was a majority owner of the Edmonton Oilers. He preferred a position with the Oilers because he and his family were hopeful of returning to Canada, especially given the tenuous financial straits that the WHA was in at that time. He said, "With or without hockey, I would feel more comfortable in Canada if I had to start over again."[227]

After meeting with Skalbania, the two men came to an agreement on a position and a contract. Brian really liked living in Indianapolis, but when the opportunity to become the general manager of the Edmonton Oilers of the WHA came along he had to jump. Brian said,

My brief time in Indianapolis aged me ten years. There was never a moment without crisis. We had enjoyed living in the US as a family, but even Susan was excited about going home to Canada. And by a stroke of luck we were able to sell our house with no real estate agent, and we got all of our money out of a house we'd lived in for less than half a year. It's ironic: the only thing that went smoothly for me in Indianapolis was my leaving.[228]

Little did Brian realize that he would face serious problems working with the Edmonton Oilers. The coach of the Oilers was Glen Sather, who had been hired by Pocklington, while Brian had been signed as GM by the other major ownership partner, Skalbania. Brian wrote: "By the time Glen and I met, the seeds of my demise were already sewn.

> In Glen's mind, I was merely the business manager, and he was, in fact if not in name yet, the general manager. I was an obstacle he had to endure until he could get rid of me and surround himself with 'his' people... The stars were aligned: Glen with Pocklington, me with Skalbania.[229]

It looked like Brian's stay with the Oilers would be short-lived, especially when Nelson Skalbania was asked to take over the Racers to keep the franchise afloat. He offered Conacher the opportunity to return to Indianapolis to run the club. Brian said that despite knowing that the loss of Nelson from the ownership team in Edmonton would probably prove to be his end with the Oilers, the financial woes of the Racers probably would also spell an end to his WHA career in short order.

At the end of his first season with the Oilers, Pocklington offered Brian a multi-year contract for the same money, but this time not as general manager but to do various other duties including scouting. Brian refused and went looking for another job.

After taking a position with a local real estate company, Conacher was invited to a meeting of the Northlands Arena board of directors. After a couple of meetings where he described the situation surrounding housing a professional hockey team, Brian was offered, and he took, the position of marketing manager of Northlands.

In May 1979 CBC television contacted Brian about providing colour commentary for Game Six of the WHA final series in Edmonton between the Oilers and Winnipeg Jets. CBC had not previously broadcast WHA games, but thinking that this might be the last WHA game ever played because of the proposed merger with the NHL, the network wanted to cover this historic moment. He accepted. After all, he had been a part of the first WHA hockey game broadcast.

Before the Oilers started their first NHL season, Ralph Mellanby from Hockey Night in Canada, contacted Brian about being part of CBC's planned broadcasts of games featuring the western Canadian teams. Conacher's response was in the positive, but Brian said that when Mellanby "ran my name up the NHL flagpole, I was still persona non grata. Whether it was a hangover from my book in 1970, my commentary in 1972, the fact I was involved with the WHA, or there was someone they liked better for the job…"[230] the job offer had to be rescinded.

In 1984 Conacher was on a trip to Toronto to visit the Royal Agricultural Winter Fair. While he was there he paid a visit to Hamilton to view the construction site of the new Copps Coliseum Arena complex. After discussions with some of the management team, he returned to Edmonton. A few days later he received a call from Hamilton's Chief Administrative Officer Lou Sage offering Brian the position of managing director and chief executive officer of the newly created Hamilton Entertainment and Convention Facilities, Inc. After some careful deliberations, Brian accepted and started his new job in the "Steel City" on January 2, 1985.

In 1989 Conacher left Hamilton to become the CEO of the Royal Agricultural Winter Fair in Toronto. After a few years with the Royal, Brian would return to his home of sorts. He was coming back to Maple Leaf Gardens, not as a player, but as an executive. In 1992 he moved into a newly created position: vice-president of building operations.

However, after Ken Dryden's appointment as President of Maple Gardens it quickly became apparent that Brian's time with the Leafs' organization was about to end.

I was confined to babysitting the Gardens until the Leafs left, at which point I would be responsible for turning out the lights and locking the doors on my way out. When you're on the outs, it's time to get out, and it was time for me to bow out of MLG and

141

the facilities management business after some fifteen years. We negotiated a mutually agreeable severance package, and at the end of January 1998, I left MLG and the Gardens and moved on to other things.[231]

Perhaps as a sense completing a full historical circle Brian attended the last Maple Leafs hockey game at Maple Leaf Gardens. On February 13, 1999…"they played the Chicago Black Hawks, the same team the Leafs played to open the building in 1931. My uncle Charlie played in that first game, and there I was at the last game. He played on the first Leafs Stanley Cup team, and I played on the last one. And in 1999, just as in 1931, the Leafs lost."[232]

In the fall of 2002 Brian became the President of the NHL Alumni Association, a position that he would hold until 2005. Perhaps there is a bit of irony in this because in the 1950s his father Lionel held position of President of the NHL Oldtimers.

Chapter Seven

<u>Murray Henderson</u>

Murray "Moe" Henderson was born September 5, 1921 in Toronto. He is one player whose connection to the Conachers is largely unknown, or ignored. Murray is the son of Dorothy Margaret "Dolly" Conacher, the eldest sibling in the Conacher family.

Growing up as part of the Conacher clan there were plenty of sports role models for a young boy to emulate. Murray chose to become a defenseman, like his uncles Lionel and Bert, rather than a forward like his uncles Charlie and Roy.

After playing hockey on the streets, backyard rinks and in youth leagues, Henderson played a season of Junior "B" hockey with Upper Canada College in 1938-39. After playing only six games and recording 2 goals and one assist, Murray left his school team and signed to play OHA Junior "A" hockey with the Toronto Young Rangers.

For the next two-and-a-half seasons, Henderson patrolled the blueline for the Young Rangers. In 44 regular season games he notched nine goals and three assists and added two more markers in eight playoff games.[233]

One of the "perks" of playing for the junior club meant getting to skate at Maple Leaf Gardens on a regular basis. He recalled that, "we used to practice at Maple Leaf Gardens at 5 in the morning. That meant we got up at 4. And we'd practice to 7 or 8, and then go to school or to work."[234][235]

He stayed in the Maple Leafs family after completing his junior career, joining the Toronto Marlboros Senior club for the 1941-42 hockey season. In 28 games he scored two goals and four assists while adding two goals and one assist in ten playoff contests.[236]

However with the Second World War impacting on all of Canadian life, in 1942 the youngster enlisted in the RCAF as a pilot. One has to wonder if this decision came about because of the influence of his uncles. Roy Conacher also joined the RCAF as a pilot, and Lionel Conacher's role in the RCAF was that of a recruiter.

Murray spent his military time in the Toronto area playing senior hockey for Toronto and Brantford RCAF hockey teams. In 1942-43, his Toronto RCAF Senior "A" club advanced all the way to Eastern Canadian Allan Cup Finals with Henderson scoring two goals and seven assists in the various preliminary playoff rounds. He registered two assists in four games before his club bowed out to the Allan Cup champs, the Ottawa Commandos.[237]

His military career came to an abrupt end late in the 1944-45 hockey season. He received an early discharge due to the death of his father.

While he left the RCAF on a sombre note, this was a time of opportunity for a young hockey player with better than average abilities. With many NHL players enlisted in the military to take part in the war effort, both at home and abroad, NHL clubs were clamouring for talent to fill out their rosters. Although he had never really considered a hockey career beyond the OHA Senior levels, Murray now found his hockey playing services in demand.

According to his obituary, it was family connections that landed him a contract with the Boston Bruins. Apparently, his uncle Charlie had approached Bruins scout "Baldy" Cotton, who was a long-time family friend of the Conachers, about signing his nephew.

And the family connections did not stop with his uncle's referral. After a three-game conditioning stint with the Bruins' farm club, the Boston Olympics of the Eastern Amateur Hockey League (EAHL), he joined the NHL club. One of his Bruins' teammates was his uncle Roy Conacher, who also had just returned from military service.

In a 1987 interview, Murray said that one of his career highlights occurred when the team was "in a bit of a slump and were playing the Rangers in Boston and I got two goals, and we won 4-1."[238] But at the same time he spoke realistically about his hockey skills and how they pertained to his stay with the Bruins:

> In those days there was the odd rushing defenseman, but most of us stayed back and guarded the blueline, and even

high-scoring defensemen would only get 10 goals a season. I was just a foot-soldier, slogging away, but in those days, each team had six or seven players who were fixtures and a lot of guys on the farm teams just waiting for the rest of us to have a bad weekend.[239]

Murray may have understated his value to the team. In the 1946-47 hockey season, he and fellow defenseman Jack Crawford were named the Bruins' alternate captains.[240] This is a role usually reserved for players who are well-respected by both their teammates and management.

Henderson remained in "Beantown" until the end of the 1951-52 NHL season. In total, he played 405 games in the National Hockey League scoring 24 goals and adding 62 assists.

Although his NHL career had come to an end, this did not mean his days in hockey were over. The 1952-53 season marked the beginning of a new era for Henderson. He joined the Hershey Bears of the American Hockey League as player-coach. For the next four seasons he would log double-duty for Bears patrolling the blueline and directing the team as the head coach. In his last season, 1955-56, he only played 9 games, before moving behind the bench for the rest of the season.

Murray was a multi-sport athlete playing baseball both as youngster and during the off-season during his hockey career. Before and after his playing career he enjoyed golf and played in charity tournaments.

The end of the 1955-56 hockey season marked the end of Murray's hockey career and the beginning of a new vocation. He joined the Seagram's company as a salesperson. He progressed through the ranks ultimately to position of Central Canadian Sales Manager.

In 1968, Murray continued his climb up the ladder of the corporate world. He accepted a position as Vice-President of Sales for the Hudson Bay brands of whiskeys, rum and gin.

Murray Henderson passed away on January 4, 2013.

Conclusion

When one takes the time to consider the number of families who have sent more than one member of their clan to the NHL, the impact of these brothers, or fathers and sons, has been significant upon the history of this great game.

Families such as Gordie Howe and has sons Mark and Marty; Maurice Richard and his brother Henri; Bobby Hull and his brother Dennis, and Bobby's son Brett; Frank Mahovlich and his brother Peter; and Eric Staal and his brothers Marc, Jordan and Jared; represent just five of the families that have made significant contributions to the game of hockey. However, there has only been one Royal Family of Hockey, the Conachers. First of all, Lionel, Charlie and Roy are the only three brothers to be inducted as Honoured Members in the Hockey Hall of Fame, not to mention all the Stanley Cup victories, All-Star appointments, scoring titles, etc. As the preceding pages illustrate the exploits of Lionel, Charlie, Roy and Bert as well as their sons Pete and Brian and their nephew Murray Henderson, there never has been a family who dominated the history of this great game like the Conachers!

Acknowledgements

There are many people to thank for their efforts in the creation this book.

John Bellamy must be thanked first of all. It was his idea that I pursue this project and his constant encouragement throughout the entire process is greatly appreciated. John also contributed many of the images used in this book. Sadly, during the final days of the production of **Hockey's Royal Family**, John passed away. This book is dedicated in his memory.

Pete Conacher, whose career and family are featured in the pages of this book was very gracious in his patiently answering questions about his life and that of his relatives.

Al Shaw and the members of the Original Six Alumni group that meets the first Monday of every month welcomed me to their gathering whenever I could attend. Talking to, and simply seeing, so many of the hockey personalities that I grew up watching provided me with ideas and the impetus to write this book.

My daughter, Tara-Lyn White, provided much-needed research assistance in this project.

John McPhee edited and provided comments and editorial assistance.

Greg Oliver, a historian of the sport of wrestling, most graciously provided a listing of Lionel Conacher's wrestling career which can be read in Appendix One.

My brother David found a research source that had eluded me.

And last, and certainly not least, my wife Judy was a constant source of encouragement. Without the support of all of these friends and family, this book might never have seen the light of day.

Appendix One

Lionel Conacher's
Wrestling Career

TORONTO, Saturday, April 16, 1932. -- (AP) – Lionel Conacher, Canada's greatest all-round athlete, announced today he was through with professional hockey and would devote his time to professional wrestling.

- Toronto, ON: Tuesday, May 3, 1932

  LIONEL CONACHER (pro debut) beat Carl Pospeshil

- Montreal, QE: Monday, May 9, 1932 at Mount Royal Arena, att.-3,500

  … Nick Lutze beat Charley Hanson (2-1) … LIONEL CONACHER beat Young Hackenschmidt … Billy Bartush beat Jack Forsgren … Marvin Westenberg drew Raoul Simon (20:00) (sub for Dan Petroff) … Yvon Robert drew Frank Judson (20:00) (sub for George Ling) … Referee: Eugene Tremblay

- Quebec City, QE: Wednesday, May 11, 1932 at arena

Billy Bartush beat Al Mercier (2-1) ... Frank Judson beat Marvin Westenberg (30:00, dec) ... Louis Loew drew Yvon Robert (15:00) ... LIONEL CONACHER vs George Link (both no showed)

■ Boston, MA: Thursday, May 12, 1932 at arena

Jim Browning beat Billy Bartush (1-1, utc) ... Charlie Strack beat Boris Demetroff ... Jack Sherry beat John Poddubny ... Count Zarynoff drew Stanley Pinto (10:00) ... Casey Kazanjian beat Kara Pasha ... Bob Wilkie drew Leo Numa (5:00) (sub for LIONEL CONACHER) ... Wong Buck Cheung drew Joe Varga (5:00) ... Charlie Hanson beat Red Smith ... Bull Martin drew Dr. Fred Meyer (5:00) ... Pat Reilly drew John Spellman (5:00)

■ Toronto, ON: Friday, May 27, 1932

Gus Sonnenberg beat Count George Zarynoff ... Joe Malcewicz beat Charlie Strack (dq) ... Sam Cordovano beat Frank Malcewicz (or lost) ... LIONEL CONACHER beat Richard Stahl

■ Windsor, ON: Wednesday, June 1, 1932

LIONEL CONACHER beat Joe Bartello (of Memphis TN) (2-0) ... Alex Kasaboski beat Bert Rubinstein (later Bert Rubi) (2-1)

■ Toronto, ON: Thursday, June 9, 1932

(World Title) Henri DeGlane* beat Joe Malcewicz (2-1) ... LIONEL CONACHER (198 pounds, Toronto) beat Eddie Elzea ... Nick Lutze beat John Spellman ... Richard Stahl beat Charles Manoogian

- Boston, MA: Wednesday, June 15, 1932 at Boston Garden – att. – 12,000

Jack Washburn beat Charlie Strack (1-1, utc) ... Referee: Ernest Roeber ... LIONEL CONACHER beat Tony Catalino ... Mike Nazarian beat Taro Miyake ... Hindu Nanjo beat Jack Burke ... George Linehan drew Fred Carone (10:00) ... Bruno Gorassini beat Tiny Ruff ... Jim Maloney drew Pat Coyne (10:00) ... Ivan Leskinovich beat Lloyd Carter ... Tiger Jack Young beat Nino Darnoldi

- Toronto, ON: Thursday, June 23, 1932

Joe Malcewicz beat Charlie Strack ... Dr. Fred Meyer beat Tony Catalino ... LIONEL CONACHER beat Louis Loew ... Sam Cordovano beat Nick Scotis

- Montreal, QE: Monday, July 4, 1932 at Mount Royal Arena

Gus Sonnenberg beat George Zarynoff ... LIONEL CONACHER vs Louis Allaire ... Joe Malcewicz vs Dr. Fred Meyer ... Jack Ganson vs Frank Judson ... Marvin Westenberg vs Raoul Simon

- Niagara Falls, ON: Wednesday, July 13, 1932

155

LIONEL CONACHER beat Tony Catalino

- Boston, MA: Thursday, July 21, 1932 at Braves Field, att. 20,000

  (WTM) Henri DeGlane* beat Jack Washburn (2-0) (first fall by dq) ... Nick Lutze drew Charlie Strack (30:00) (sub for Jack Sherry) ... Jim Browning drew Ed Don George (15:00) ... Len Macaluso drew Joe Malcewicz (10:00) ... Pat McGill drew Al Morelli (10:00) ... Casey Kazanjian beat Len Frisbee ... Lee Wykoff beat Tiny Ruff ... John Spellman drew Charlie Hanson (10:00) ... LIONEL CONACHER beat Bill Nelson ... Bull Martin drew Buck Weaver (10:00) ... Harry Cornsweet beat Rex Smith ... Referees: Ted Tonneman and Charley Donnell

- Montreal, QE: Thursday, August 4, 1932 at Royals Stadium

  Sammy Stein beat Howard Cantonwine (2-1, dq) ... Masked Marvel beat Scotty McDougal ... Dr. Ralph Wilson drew George Hagen (30:00) ... LIONEL CONACHER beat Richard Stahl ... Maurice Letchford beat Don Stockton ... Referee: Jimmie McKimmie

- Buffalo, NY: August 12, 1932 at Bison Stadium

  Joe Malcewicz beat Regis Siki ... Bibber McCoy beat Len Macaluso (dec) ... Fred Meyer beat Karol Nowina ... Art Mayer beat Carl Lemle ... Eddie Elzea drew John Gonda ...

NOTE: LIONEL CONACHER vs Hans Schroeder (no shows)

About The Author

Paul White

Paul White is a long time hockey historian and sports biographer. His books and articles have included stories about many of the great hockey players of the past and present. He has written about Willie O'Ree the first African American to play in the NHL, Rocket Richard, Henri Richard, Alex Delvecchio, Sid Abel, Teeder Kennedy, Syl Apps, Max Bentley, Jean Beliveau, Milt Schmidt, Harry Lumley, Paul Henderson the scoring star of the 1972 Canada-Russia Super Series and many other hockey legends. Although he is a noted hockey historian Paul White has also written about hockey players who are still currently skating in the NHL including

Pittsburgh Penguins super star Sidney Crosby, Brad Richards, Boston Bruins super pest, Brad Marchand and many more.

Other Books By

<u>Paul White</u>

- **Shooting For The Moon: The Bill Beagan Story**, Amazon

- **East Coast NHLers**, Formac

- **Great Centremen: Stars of Hockey's Golden Age**, Altitude

- **How to Collect Sports Cards for Fun and Profit**, Amazon

- **Owen Sound: the Port City**, Natural Heritage/Dundurn

- **The Fastest Driving Route to Florida**, Amazon

Resources

Interviews:

- "Ace" Bailey, various occasions, 1989-90

- Pete Conacher – March 7, 2014 by telephone

Bibliography

1/ Articles

- Albert, Norman; "Conacher Scores Six For North Toronto, **Toronto Daily Star**, February 9, 1923, pg. 12

- Beddoes, Dick; "Foster Hewitt Turns Back the Clock", **Hockey Pictorial**, December 1958, pp. 20,21 and 30

- Burnett, Red; "Money, Big Money, is Key to Brian's Hockey Future", **Toronto Daily Star**, September 18, 1965, pg. 40

- Conacher, Roy; "The Goal I'll Never Forget", **Blueline Magazine**, December 1957, pg. 5

- Cowie, Don; "Dominions Beat Sudbury, 4-2, and Square Series", **Globe and Mail**, March 27, 1937, pg. 18

- "Boston and Rangers Mangle Lowly Opponents: R. Conacher Ties Record", **Globe and Mail**, February 22, 1937, pg. 17

- Fitkin, Ed; "The Gashouse Gang of Hockey", **Maple Leaf Gardens** program, January 20, 1965, pp. 58-70

- Gamester, George; "Toronto's First Family of Hockey", **Toronto Star**, November 23, 2003, pg. A17

- Goodhand, Glen R.; "First Game, First Shift, First Goal!", **The Hockey Research Journal**, Society for International Hockey Research, Volume XVI, 2012/13

- Hewitt, W.A.; "Sporting Views and Reviews", **Toronto Daily Star**, September 21, 1931, pg. 10

- Hunt, Jim; "A Conacher in Argos Future", **Toronto Daily Star**, May 31, 1961, pg. 25

- McKee, Ken; "Brian Tops Uncle Charlie", **Toronto Star**, October 24, 1966, pg. 12

- McKenzie, Ken; "Camera in the Corridor – King Clancy", **Hockey Pictorial**, December 1956, pg. 34

- Lytle, Andy; "Pushing the Puck Around", **Toronto Star**, November 12, 1936, pg. 17

- Lytle, Andy; "Starry Company Threaten to Retire as Season Ends", **Toronto Daily Star**, March 16, 1937, pg. 12

- Lytle, Andy; "Speaking on Sports". **Toronto Daily Star**, January 9, 1946, pg. 8

- MacLean, Norman; "Ten Greatest Cup Games", **Hockey Illustrated**, Volume 7, Number 7, May 1968, pg. 41

- Marks, Jack; "Golf", **Globe and Mail**, May 27, 1966, pg. 29

- Marsh, Lou; "Did Conacher Beat Hamilton Tigers", **Toronto Daily Star**, October 16, 1922, pg. 9

- Marsh, Lou; "With Pick and Shovel", **Toronto Daily Star**, October 22, 1931, pg. 16

- Munns, Tommy; "Lionel Conacher Favored as NHL Referee-in-Chief", **Globe and Mail**, September 13, 1938, pg. 17

- Nickleson, Al; "Hawks Push Referee as Leafs Gain 6-3 Win", **Globe and Mail**, February 5, 1951, pg. 21

- Obodiac, Stan; "Brian Conacher: No Hockey Brat He", **Hockey Pictorial**, December 1967, pg. 36

- Patton, Paul; "Where Are They Now? – Murray Henderson", **Globe and Mail**, September 19, 1987, pg. F4

- Proudfoot, Jim; "Another Piece Added to Conacher Legend", **Toronto Star**, November 16, 1998, pg. E7

- Proudfoot, Jim; "Howe is Happy to Emulate Idol", **Toronto Star**, December 24, 1963, pg. 9

- Roche, Bill; "Conacher's Two Goals Beat Leafs", **Globe and Mail**, April 14, 1939, pg. 18

- Scott, Margaret; "Where Are They Now? – Roy Conacher", **Hockey Pictorial**, February 1960, pg. 32 and 36

- Shea, Kevin; "Legends of Hockey – Spotlight – Lionel Conacher", Hockey Hall of Fame, January 30, 2006

- Shea, Kevin; "Spotlight: One on One with Charlie Conacher", Hockey Hall of Fame, 2011

- Smith, Wilf; "Conacher is Surprised by NHL Leafs' Draft, Cites 'A Poor Season'," **Globe and Mail**, June 5, 1957, pg. 18

- Thompson, Jimmy; "The Oddest Goal Scored This Year", **Toronto Daily Star**, December 8, 1930, pg. 12

- Vipond, Jim; "Campbell Says Hugh McLean Acted Rightly", **Globe and Mail**, February 6, 1951

- Walker, Hal; "Full House Greets NHL Old-Timers at Bracebridge", **Globe and Mail**, January 26, 1952, pg. 17

- Young, Jerry; "Conacher is a Big Train as UCC Edges Trinity, 13-11", **Toronto Daily Star**, Nov. 1, 1954, pg. 19

- "Bauer Appointed Bruins' Captain", **Globe and Mail**, October 17, 1946, pg. 18

- "Big Train Gathers Plenty Steam To Push Pro Football in Canada"; **Toronto Daily Star**, July 25, 1933, pg. 10

- "Big Train's Son Wins Five Events in Meet at UCC", **Globe and Mail**, May 23, 1951, pg. 19

- "Boston and Rangers Mangle Lowly Opponents: R. Conacher Ties Record", **Globe and Mail**, Feb, 22, 1937, pg. 17

- "Bowsers to Tangle With Leaders", **Globe and Mail**, December 8, 1945, pg. 17

- "Canada's Greatest Athlete", **Toronto Daily Star**, May 28, 1954, pg. 6

- "Canadiens Want Lionel Conacher", **Globe and Mail**, December 25, 1920, pg. 8

- "Century Polls Go Amiss", **Toronto Star**, December 2, 1999, pg. B8

- "Conacher and Burch to Open Clothing Store", **Toronto Daily Star**, April 5, 1922, pg. 19

- "Conacher to Make Personal Appeal", **Globe and Mail**, November 7, 1925, pg. 13

- "Conacher Fund Set Up to Fight Cancer", **Toronto Star**, January 2, 1968, pg. 13

- "Conacher is Serious", **Toronto Daily Star**, September 19, 1933, pg. 6

- "Conacher Quits Rink for Political Arena", **Toronto Daily Star**, September 2, 1937, pg. 47

- "Conachers Take Sports-Day Titles", **Globe and Mail**, June 2, 1945, pg. 17

- "Conny Stars But Arpeaks Again Outplay the Chefs", **Toronto Daily Star**, October 14, 1933, pg. 8

- "Hamilton Refuses to Play Against Lionel Conacher", **Globe and Mail**, November 13, 1923, pg. 12

- "Hawks Eclipse Bruins 7-5, Roy Conacher Tallies 3", **Globe and Mail**, March 23, 1950, pg. 19

- "Jesse Ketchum Team Whips Old Boys 5-2", **Globe and Mail**, June 19, 1936, pg. 7

- "Kicking the Puck Around", **Toronto Daily Star**, January 29, 1935, pg. 8

- "Conacher to Make Personal Appeal", **Globe and Mail**, November 7, 1925, pg. 13

- "Lacrosse, Bike Sprints and Wrestling Go On Air", **Toronto Daily Star**, May 3, 1932, pg. 22

- "L. Conacher's Broad Shoulders Prove Great Help To

Premier", **Toronto Daily Star**, October 6, 1937, pg. 36

■ "Little Train No. 2 Arrives on Scene", **Toronto Daily Star**, January 8, 1936, pg. 8

■ "Many Athletes Frown on Sons Taking Up Game", **Toronto Daily Star**, July 23, 1937, pg. 24

■ "Men's Police Court", **Toronto Daily Star**, June 29, 1927, pg. 4

■ "New Faces Fail to Help Fuels as Uptowns Romp to 11-3 Win", **Globe and Mail**, February 5. 1945, pg. 14

■ "OLA Champs to Get Conacher Memorial"; **Toronto Daily Star**, May 8, 1955, pg. 14

■ "Only Liberal Policies Can Aid Trade – Pearson", **Toronto Daily Star**, May 18, 1949, pg. 12

■ "Pete Conacher Replaces Uncle Roy at Left Wing with Black Hawks", **Globe and Mail**, November 17, 1951, pg. 18

■ "Pete Conacher Chip Off the Old Block", **Toronto Daily Star**, September 27, 1952, pg. 20

■ "Pete Conacher Shines", **Globe and Mail**, October 31, 1952, pg. 16

■ "Peter Conacher Raps 3 Goals; Hawks Win, 7-0", **Globe and Mail**, March 20, 1954, pg. 20

- "Pete Conacher Scores 3 Goals in Hershey Win", **Globe and Mail**, February 6, 1964, pg. 26

- "Pro Hockey Stars in Huntsville Tilt", **Globe and Mail**, August 12, 1941, pg. 14

- "Random Notes on Current Sports", **Toronto Daily Star**, May 15, 1922, pg. 8

- "Ross is Pleased With Candidates", **Globe and Mail**, October 24, 1935, pg. 7

- "Roy Conacher Still Unsigned; Now in Toronto", **Globe and Mail**, October 17, 1947, pg. 15

- "Roy Conacher Retires from Pro Hockey Scene", **Globe and Mail**, October 28, 1947, pg. 18

- "Roy Conacher Winner in NHL Point Derby", **Globe and Mail**, March 21, 1949, pg. 19

- "Stop! Look! Listen!" **Toronto Daily Star**, April 15, 1932, pg. 10

- "The Buck Attacks on Conacher", **Toronto Star**, June 24, 1949

- "The Youngest Line", **Blueline Magazine**, January 1958, pg. 17

- "Tommy Gorman Predicts Big Things for Lionel", **Toronto**

Daily Star, September 16, 1937, pg. 17

2/ Books

- Batten, Jack and George Johnson, Bob Duff, Steve Milton, Lance Hornby; **Hockey Dynasties: Blue Lines and Blood Lines**, Firefly Books, Buffalo, NY, 2002

- Conacher, Brian; **Hockey in Canada: The Way It Is!**, Gateway Press, Toronto, 1970

- Conacher, Brian; **As The Puck Turns: A Personal Journey Through the World of Hockey**, Harper Collins Canada Ltd., Toronto, 2007

- Cox, Damien & Gord Stellick; **'67: The Leafs, Their Sensational Victory, and the end of an Empire**, John Wiley & Sons Canada Ltd., Toronto, 2004

- Dryden, Steve, editor; **The Top 100 NHL Players of All Time**, McClelland & Stewart Inc, Toronto, 1998

- Duplacey, James and Charles Wilkins; **Forever Rivals: Montreal Canadiens – Toronto Maple Leafs**, Random House of Canada, Toronto, 1996

- Hockey Hall of Fame; **Legends of Hockey**, Penguin Books, Toronto, 1996

- Hunter, Douglas; **Open Ice: The Tim Horton Story**, Penguin Books, Toronto, 1995

- Irvin, Dick; **In the Crease: Goaltenders Look at Life in the NHL**, McClelland & Stewart, Toronto, 1995

- Lapp, Richard M. & Alec Macaulay; **The Memorial Cup: Canada's National Junior Hockey Championship**, Harbour Publishing, Madeira Park, British Columbia, 1997

- McAllister, Ron; **Hockey Stars: today and yesterday**, McClelland and Stewart, Toronto, 1950, pg. 19

- McFarlane, Brian; **Stanley Cup Fever**, Stoddart Publishing Company Limited, Toronto, 1992

- Obodiac, Stan; **Maple Leaf Gardens: Fifty Years of History**, Van Nostrand Reinhold Ltd. Toronto, 1981

- Pelletier, Joe; "Pete Conacher", blackhawkslegends.blogspot.ca, August 2008

- Pelletier, Joe; "Brian Conacher", mapleleaflegends.blogspot.ca, 2007

- Pelletier, Joe; "Charlie Conacher", mapleleaflegends.blogspot.ca, April 2008

- Pelletier, Joe; "Lionel Conacher", montrealmaroons.blogspot.ca, April 2008

- Shea, Kevin; **Spotlight: One on One with Lionel Conacher**, Hockey Hall of Fame, Toronto, 2006

- Shea, Kevin with Paul Patskou, Roly Harris, & Paul Bruno; **Toronto Maple Leafs: Diary of a Dynasty 1957-1967**, Firefly, Toronto, 2010

- Smythe, Conn with Scott Young; **Conn Smythe: If You Can't Beat 'Em in the Alley**, McClelland & Stewart, Toronto, 1981

- Young, Scott; **Hello Canada! The Life and Times of Foster Hewitt**, McClelland & Stewart Bantam Ltd., Toronto, 1985

3/ Radio Interviews:

- Brian Conacher interview on Ontario Morning on CBC Radio, February 13, 2014[241]

Endnotes

[1] Proudfoot, Jim; "Another Piece Added to Conacher Legend", **Toronto Star**, November 11, 1998, pg. E7

[2] Proudfoot, Jim; "Another Piece Added to Conacher Legend", **Toronto Star**, November 11, 1998, pg. E7

[3] Benjamin was born in Petrolia, Ontario in 1870, the son of William Conacher, who arrived in Canada from Scotland sometime after his birth in 1841 and 1843, and Helen Maria Manners Young.

[4] Elizabeth was born in Dublin, Ireland in 1872 and it is not known when she arrived in Canada.

[5] The 5 girls were Victoria (Queenie), Dorothy (Dolly), Mary, and the twins, Nora and Kathleen (Kay). The 5 boys were Lionel, Dermot, Charlie, and the twins, Bert and Roy.

[6] They lived on Davenport Road, Bishop Street, Berryman Street, Northview, McMurrich Street, and Dupont Street.

[7] Charlie Conacher quote from a 1936 Maclean's Magazine article

[8] Gamester, George; "Toronto's First Family of Hockey", **Toronto Star**, November 23, 2003, pg. A17

[9] Shea, Kevin; **One on One with Lionel Conacher**, HHoF, 2006

[10] "Canada's Greatest Athlete", **Toronto Daily Star**, May 28, 1954, pg. 6

[11] Shea, Kevin; "Spotlight: One on One With Lionel Conacher", Hockey Hall of Fame, January 30, 2006

[12] He had won several titles as a youngster playing in various age-group categories of sports other than hockey.

[13] Society for International Hockey Research (SIHR) Database

[14] Marsh, Lou; Did Conacher Beat the Hamilton Tigers", **Toronto Daily Star**, October 16, 1922 pg. 9

[15] Marsh, Lou; Did Conacher Beat the Hamilton Tigers", **Toronto Daily Star**, October 16, 1922 pg. 9

[16] In 1923 Lionel had taken a dramatic step in his career path. Surprising both friends and family, he changed his placed of residence. Not only did he leave home, but he also left not only his hometown, but Canada! In what one Toronto newspaper called "one of the Yankees' greatest victories since the War of Independence", Conacher moved to Pittsburgh, Pennsylvania to play hockey and football, and, perhaps more importantly, improve his education. (Reported by Kevin Shea in a 2006 Hockey Hall of Fame article entitled "One on One with Lionel Conacher".

[17] "Hamilton Refuses to Play Against Lionel Conacher", **Globe and Mail**, November 13, 1923, pg. 12

[18] "Conacher to Make Personal Appeal", **Globe and Mail**, November 7, 1925, pg.

13

[19] Shea, Kevin; "One-on-One with Lionel Conacher, Hockey Hall of Fame, January 30, 2006

[20] "Canadiens Want Lionel Conacher", **Globe and Mail**, December 25, 1920, pg. 8

[21] "Canadiens Want Lionel Conacher", **Globe and Mail**, December 25, 1920, pg. 8

[22] Shea, Kevin, "Spotlight – One on One With Lionel Conacher", Hockey Hall of Fame, January 30, 2006

[23] Craig Campbell, Manager Hockey Hall of Fame Resource Centre, March 14, 2014

[24] "Random Notes on Current Sports", **Toronto Daily Star**, May 15, 1922, pg. 8

[25] Albert, Norman; "Conacher Scores Six For North Toronto, **Toronto Daily Star**, February 9, 1923, pg. 12

[26] Walker, Hal; "Full House Greets NHL Old-Timers at Bracebridge", **Globe and Mail**, January 26, 1952, pg. 17

[27] "Conacher and Burch to Open Clothing Store", **Toronto Daily Star**, April 5, 1922, pg. 19

[28] "Conacher and Burch to Open Clothing Store", **Toronto Daily Star**, April 5, 1922, pg. 19

[29] Harold Darragh, Herb Drury, Frank McCurry, Hib Milks, Dalton Meeking, Rodger Smith, Tex White all were Canadians born in the province of Ontario.

[30] Shea, Kevin; One on One with Lionel Conacher, HHoF, 2006

[31] One of Lionel's teammates with the baseball Maple Leafs was Carl Hubbell, a pitcher who would go on to a Hall of Fame baseball career with the New York Giants.

[32] Shea, Kevin; One on One with Lionel Conacher, HHoF, 2006

[33] Shea, Kevin; One on One with Lionel Conacher, HHoF, 2006

[34] Shea, Kevin; One on One with Lionel Conacher, HHoF, 2006

[35] "Men's Police Court", **Toronto Daily Star**, June 29, 1927, pg. 4

[36] "Lacrosse Chatter" **Toronto Daily Star**, July 22, 1930, pg. 8

[37] Shea, Kevin, "One on One with Lionel Conacher" Hockey Hall of Fame, 2006

[38] Hewitt, W.A.; "Sporting Views and Reviews" **Toronto Daily Star**, September 21, 1931, pg. 10

[39] For a partial listing of the results from Conacher's wrestling matches see Appendix One

[40] "Kicking the Puck Around", **Toronto Daily Star**, January 29, 1935, pg. 8

[41] "Big Train Gathers Plenty Steam To Push Pro Football in Canada" **Toronto Daily Star**, July 25, 1933, pg. 10

[42] "Big Train Gathers Plenty Steam To Push Pro Football in Canada" **Toronto Daily Star**, July 25, 1933, pg. 10

[43] "Conny Stars But Arpeaks Again Outplay the Chefs", **Toronto Daily Star**, October 14, 1933, pg. 8

[44] "Conny Stars But Arpeaks Again Outplay the Chefs", **Toronto Daily Star**,

October 14, 1933, pg. 8

[45] Shea, Kevin, "One on One With Lionel Conacher" Hockey Hall of Fame, January 30, 2006

[46] Lytle, Andy; "Pushing the Puck Around", **Toronto Daily Star**, November 12, 1936, pg. 17

[47] "Conacher Quits Rink for Political Arena", **Toronto Daily Star**, September 2, 1937, pg. 47

[48] "Tommy Gorman Predicts Big Things for Lionel", **Toronto Daily Star**, September 16, 1937, pg. 17

[49] "L. Conacher's Broad Shoulders Prove Great Help To Premier", **Toronto Daily Star**, October 6, 1937, pg. 36

[50] Munns, Tommy; "Lionel Conacher Favored as NHL Referee-in-Chief", **Globe and Mail**, September 13, 1938, pg. 17

[51] Munns, Tommy; "Lionel Conacher Favored as NHL Referee-in-Chief", **Globe and Mail**, September 13, 1938, pg. 17

[52] Munns, Tommy; "Lionel Conacher Favored as NHL Referee-in-Chief", **Globe and Mail**, September 13, 1938, pg. 17

[53] Munns, Tommy; "Lionel Conacher Favored as NHL Referee-in-Chief", **Globe and Mail**, September 13, 1938, pg. 17

[54] The Election Expenses published in the **Toronto Daily Star** on October 14, 1949 reveals that another Conacher had a significant role in Lionel's campaign. His sister Nora was listed as the Official Agent of his campaign.

[55] The Communist Party of Canada was also known as the Labour Progressive Party for much of the 1940s and 1950s.

[56] "The Buck Attacks on Conacher", **Toronto Star**, June 24, 1949

[57] "Only Liberal Policies Can Aid Trade – Pearson", **Toronto Daily Star**, May 18, 1949, pg. 12

[58] "OLA Champs to Get Conacher Memorial"; **Toronto Daily Star**, May 8, 1955, pg. 14

[59] Proudfoot, Jim; "Howe is Happy to Emulate Idol", **Toronto Star**, December 24, 1963, pg. 9

[60] "Century Polls Go Amiss", **Toronto Star**, December 2, 1999, pg. B8

[61] "Little Train No. 2 Arrives on Scene", **Toronto Daily Star,** January 8, 1936, pg. 8

[62] Cox, Damien and Gord Stellick, **'67: The Leafs, Their Sensational Victory, and the end of an Empire,** John Wiley & Sons Canada Ltd., Toronto, 2004, pg. 237

[63] "Conachers Take Sports-Day Titles", **Globe and Mail**, June 2, 1945, pg. 17

[64] "Big Train's Son Wins Five Events in Meet at UCC", **Globe and Mail**, May 23, 1951, pg. 19

[65] Young, Jerry; "Conacher is a Big Train as UCC Edges Trinity, 13-11", **Toronto Daily Star**, November 1, 1954, pg. 19

[66] Hunt, Jim; "A Conacher in Argos Future", **Toronto Daily Star**, May 31, 1961, pg. 25

[67]Batten, Jack and George Johnson, Bob Duff, Steve Milton, Lance Hornby; **Hockey Dynasties: Blue Lines and Bloodlines**, Firefly Books, Buffalo, 2002, pg. 34

[68]Dryden: **The Top 100**, pg. 100

[69] McAllister, Ron; **Hockey Stars: today and yesterday**, McClelland and Stewart, Toronto, 1950, pg. 19

[70] Lapp, Richard M. & Alec Macaulay; **The Memorial Cup: Canada's National Junior Hockey Championship**, Harbour Publishing, Madeira Park, British Columbia, 1997, pg. 35

[71]Conacher, Brian; **Hockey in Canada: The Way It Is!**, Gateway Press, Toronto, 1970, pg. 11

[72]Goodhand, Glen R.; "First Game, First Shift, First Goal!", **The Hockey Research Journal**, Society for International Hockey Research Volume XVI, 2012/13, pg. 146

[73]Not long after his arrival in Toronto, Jackson would be tagged with the nickname "Busher".

[74]According to author Richard M. Lapp, This was not the first moniker that Jackson and Conacher had played under. As members of the 1929 Memorial Cup Champion Toronto Marlboros Conacher, and Jackson played on a line with centre Eddie Convey called the "Three Musketeers".

[75] "The Youngest Line", **Blueline Magazine**, January 1958, pg. 17

[76] McAllister, Ron; **Hockey Stars**, pg. 21

[77] Thompson, Jimmy; "The Oddest Goal Scored This Year", **Toronto Daily Star**, December 8, 1930, pg. 12

[78] Marsh, Lou; "With Pick and Shovel", **Toronto Daily Star**, October 22, 1931, pg. 16

[79] Bert Conacher told George Gamester in a 2003 interview that Charlie was not the only Conacher to witness the opening   night of Maple Leaf Gardens in person. His younger brothers Bert and Roy were working in the stands selling programs for the inaugural game.

[80] Fitkin, Ed; "The Gashouse Gang of Hockey", **Maple Leaf Gardens** program, January 20, 1965, pp. 59-60

[81] Fitkin, Ed; "The Gashouse Gang of Hockey", **Maple Leaf Gardens** program, January 20, 1965, pg. 62

[82] "Stop! Look! Listen!" **Toronto Daily Star**, April 15, 1932, pg. 10

[83]Irvin, Dick; **In the Crease: Goaltenders Look at Life in the NHL**, McClelland & Stewart, Toronto, 1995, pg. 316

[84] Fitkin, Ed; "The Gashouse Gang of Hockey", Maple Leaf Gardens program, January 20, 1965, pg. 62

[85] McFarlane, Brian; **Stanley Cup Fever**, Stoddart Publishing Company Limited, Toronto, 1992, pg. 78

[86] "Conacher is Serious", **Toronto Daily Star**, September 19, 1933, pg. 6

[87] Cox, Damien & Gord Stellick; **'67: The Leafs, Their Sensational Victory, and the end of an Empire**, John Wiley & Sons Canada Ltd., Toronto, 2004, pg. 106

[88] Smythe, Conn; **If You Can't Beat 'Em in the Alley**, pg. 98

[89] Smythe, Conn; **If You Can't Beat 'Em in the Alley**, pg. 109

[90] Fitkin, Ed; "The Gashouse Gang of Hockey", **Maple Leaf Gardens** program, January 20, 1965, pp. 62-64

[91] Smythe, Conn; **If You Can't Beat 'Em in the Alley**, pg. 123

[92] Smythe, Conn; **If You Can't Beat 'Em in the Alley**, pg. 137

[93] McAllister, Ron; **Hockey Stars**, pg. 22

[94] Shea, Kevin; "Spotlight: One on One with Charlie Conacher", Hockey Hall of Fame, 2011

[95] Pelletier, Joe; "Charlie Conacher", mapleleaflegends.blogspot.ca, April 2008

[96] Batten, etal; **Hockey Dynasties**, pg. 104

[97] Pelletier; mapleleaflegends.blogspot.ca

[98] McAllister, Ron; **Hockey Stars**, pg. 18

[99] Cox & Stellick pg. 236

[100] Dryden, Steve, editor; **The Top 100 NHL Players of All Time**, McClelland & Stewart Inc, Toronto, 1998, pg. 100

[101] Dryden; **The Top 100**, pg. 100

[102] In 2014 "Teeder" Kennedy was recognized as one of the all-time great Maple Leafs when he was the first player chosen to appear in the "All-Time Leafs" statue that the club was erecting at the Air Canada Centre.

[103] Hockey Hall of Fame; **Legends of Hockey**, Penguin Books, Toronto, 1996, pg. 88

[104] Young, Scott; **Hello Canada! The Life and Times of Foster Hewitt**, McClelland & Stewart Bantam Ltd., Toronto, 1985, pg. 59

[105] Young, Scott; **Hello Canada!**, pg. 60

[106] Young, Scott, **Hello Canada!**, pg. 106

[107]"Ace" Bailey interviews with the author, 1989-1990

[108] Fitkin, Ed; "The Gashouse Gang of Hockey", **Maple Leaf Gardens** program, January 20, 1965, pg. 64

[109] McKenzie, Ken; "Camera in the Corridor – King Clancy", **Hockey Pictorial**, December 1956, pg. 34

[110]Hunter, Douglas; **Open Ice: The Tim Horton Story**, Penguin Books, Toronto, 1995, pg. 549

[111] Beddoes, Dick; "Foster Hewitt Turns Back the Clock", **Hockey Pictorial**, December 1958, pp. 20,21 and 30

[112]Charlie's selection to the 1933-34 NHL First All-Star Team and his brother Lionel's selection as a First All-Star defenseman marked the first time that brothers had been selected to the NHL's First Team.

[113] Duplacey, James and Joseph Romain; **Toronto Maple Leafs: Images of Glory**, McGraw-Hill Ryerson, Toronto, 1990, pg.33

[114] McAllister, Ron; **Hockey Stars**, pg. 23

[115] Lytle, Andy; "Starry Company Threaten to Retire as Season Ends", **Toronto Daily Star**, March 16, 1937, pg. 12

[116] McAllister, Ron; **Hockey Stars**, pg. 22

[117] McFarlane, Brian; **Stanley Cup Fever**, Stoddart Publishing Company Limited, Toronto, 1992, pg. 109

[118] "Pro Hockey Stars in Huntsville Tilt", **Globe and Mail**, August 12, 1941, pg. 14

[119] Gamester, George; "Toronto's First Family of Hockey", **Toronto Star**, November 23, 2003, pg. A17

[120] "Conacher Fund Set Up to Fight Cancer", **Toronto Star**, January 2, 1968, pg. 13

[121] Duplacey, James and Charles Wilkins; **Forever Rivals: Montreal Canadiens – Toronto Maple Leafs**, Random House of Canada, Toronto, 1996, pg. 43

[122]Shea, Kevin with Paul Patskou, Roly Harris, & Paul Bruno; **Toronto Maple Leafs: Diary of a Dynasty 1957-1967**, Firefly, Toronto, 2010, pg. 352

[123]Obodiac, Stan; **Maple Leaf Gardens: Fifty Years of History**, Van Nostrand Reinhold Ltd. Toronto, 1981, pg. 99

[124] Cox and Stellick; **67**, pg. 238

[125]This wing has since been replaced with the MaRS Building.

[126]Shea, Kevin; **One on One with Charlie Conacher**, Hockey Hall of Fame, February 4, 2011

[127]Awarded between 1968 and 1984

[128]Shea; **One on One with Charlie Conacher**

[129] In 1988 The NHL replaced the Charlie Conacher Award with the King Clancy Memorial Award.

[130] Batten, etc.; **Hockey Dynasties**, pg. 41

[131] Gamester, George; "Toronto's First Family of Hockey", **Toronto Star**, November 23, 2003, pg. A17

[132] Gamester, George; "Toronto's First Family of Hockey", **Toronto Star**, November 23, 2003, pg. A17

[133] "Bowsers to Tangle With Leaders", **Globe and Mail**, December 8, 1945, pg. 17

[134] Gamester, George; "Toronto's First Family of Hockey", **Toronto Star**, November 23, 2003, pg. A17

[135] "Jesse Ketchum Team Whips Old Boys 5-2", **Globe and Mail**, June 19, 1936, pg. 7

[136] Marks, Jack; "Golf", **Globe and Mail**, May 27, 1966, pg. 29

[137] "Roy Conacher Still Unsigned; Now in Toronto", **Globe and Mail**, October 17, 1947, pg. 15

[138] Conacher, Brian; **Hockey in Canada: The Way It Is!,** Gateway Press, Toronto, 1970, pg. 13

[139] "Ross is Pleased With Candidates", **Globe and Mail**, October 24, 1935, pg. 7

[140] Twin brother Bert was also a member of the Memorial Cup Champion West Toronto Nationals

[141] Cowie, Don; "Dominions Beat Sudbury, 4-2, and Square Series", **Globe and Mail**, March 27, 1937, pg. 18

[142] "Boston and Rangers Mangle Lowly Opponents: R. Conacher Ties Record", **Globe and Mail**, February 22, 1937, pg. 17

[143] "Frankie Brimsek Voted Best Rookie of Season", **Globe and Mail**, March 30, 1939, pg. 16

[144] MacLean, Norman; "Ten Greatest Cup Games", **Hockey Illustrated**, Volume 7, Number 7, May 1968, pg. 41

[145] Roche, Bill; "Conacher's Two Goals Beat Leafs", **Globe and Mail**, April 14, 1939, pg. 18

[146] Conacher, Roy; "The Goal I'll Never Forget", **Blueline Magazine**, December 1957, pg. 5

[147] Conacher, Roy; "The Goal I'll Never Forget", **Blueline Magazine**, December 1957, pg. 5

[148] Scott, Margaret; "Where Are They Now? – Roy Conacher", **Hockey Pictorial**, February 1960, pg. 32

[149] "Roy Conacher Still Unsigned; Now in Toronto", **Globe and Mail**, October 17, 1947, pg. 15

[150] "Roy Conacher Retires from Pro Hockey Scene", **Globe and Mail**, October 28, 1947, pg. 18

[151] During the 1940s and 1950s when a player refused to sign a contract or any way

181

threatened the "status quo", NHL general manager like Adams and Toronto's Conn Smythe often, it seemed, dealt these players to Chicago.

[152] For some reason, in the 1940s and 1950s when a player refused a trade or generally disobeyed his team's bosses, they were traded to Chicago. At that time, the Black Hawks were considered to be the doormats of the NHL and not a favourable destination for most hockey players.

[153] Scott, Margaret; "Where Are They Now? – Roy Conacher", **Hockey Pictorial**, February 1960, pg. 36

[154] "Roy Conacher Winner in NHL Point Derby", **Globe and Mail**, March 21, 1949, pg. 19

[155] "Hawks Eclipse Bruins 7-5, Roy Conacher Tallies 3", **Globe and Mail**, March 23, 1950, pg. 19

[156] Nickleson, Al; "Hawks Push Referee as Leafs Gain 6-3 Win", **Globe and Mail**, February 5, 1951, pg. 21

[157] Vipond, Jim; "Campbell Says Hugh McLean Acted Rightly", **Globe and Mail**, February 6, 1951

[158] Conacher, Brian; **Hockey in Canada**, pg. 13

[159] Proudfoot, Jim; "Another Piece Added to Conacher Legend", **Toronto Star**, November 11, 1998, pg. E7

[160] "Bobby" was Pete's mother's nickname, her real name was Noreen.

[161] Interview with the author, March 7, 2014

[162] Pelletier, Joe; "Pete Conacher", blackhawkslegends.blogspot.ca, August 2008

[163] Smith went on to an NHL career with the Boston Bruins from 1944 to 1951

[164] Tilson joined the Canadian war effort after graduating from junior hockey and sadly was killed in action at the age of 20 on October 27, 1944

[165] Pete Conacher interview with author March 7, 2014

[166] Pete Conacher interview with author March 7, 2014

[167] When Roy Conacher returned from military service he played 4 games at the end of the 1945-46 NHL season and a further 3 games in the playoffs that year.

[168] Pete Conacher interview with author March 7, 2014

[169] Line mate Ken Wharram notched an almost equally impressive 114 scoring points.

[170] "Pete Conacher Replaces Uncle Roy at Left Wing with Black Hawks", **Globe and Mail**, November 17, 1951, pg. 18

[171] "Pete Conacher Replaces Uncle Roy at Left Wing with Black Hawks", **Globe and Mail**, November 17, 1951, pg. 18

[172] "Pete Conacher Chip Off the Old Block", **Toronto Daily Star**, September 27, 1952, pg. 20

[173] At that time the Stanley Cup Play-offs consisted of two play-off series. The Red Wings swept Toronto 4-0 in the semi-finals and then swept the Montreal Canadiens in the final round. They were the only team to ever accomplish this feat.

[174] "Pete Conacher Shines", **Globe and Mail**, October 31, 1952, pg. 16

[175] "Pete Conacher Raps 3 Goals; Hawks Win, 7-0", **Globe and Mail**, March 20, 1954, pg. 20

[176] Smith, Wilf; "Conacher is Surprised by NHL Leafs' Draft, Cites 'A Poor Season'," **Globe and Mail**, June 5, 1957, pg. 18

[177] Smith, Wilf; "Conacher is Surprised by NHL Leafs' Draft, Cites 'A Poor Season'," **Globe and Mail**, June 5, 1957, pg. 18

[178] Smith, Wilf; "Conacher is Surprised by NHL Leafs' Draft, Cites 'A Poor Season'," **Globe and Mail**, June 5, 1957, pg. 18

[179] Pelletier; blackhawkslegends.blogspot.ca

[180] Pete Conacher interview with author March 7, 2014

[181] Pelletier; blackhawkslegends.blogspot.ca

[182] In 1961-62 he notched 27 goals and 29 assists; 1962-63 he recorded 29 goals and 24 assists; 1963-64 saw Pete break the 30-goal plateau with 34 goals and 26 assists; and the next year, 1964-65 he fired 34 goals and added 24 assists.

[183] "Pete Conacher Scores 3 Goals in Hershey Win", Globe and Mail, February 6, 1964, pg. 26

[184] Pete Conacher interview with author March 7, 2014

[185] Pelletier; blackhawkslegends.blogspot.ca

[186] McKee, Ken; "Brian Tops Uncle Charlie", **Toronto Star**, October 24, 1966, pg. 12

[187] Conacher, Brian; **Hockey in Canada**, pg. 13

[188] Conacher, Brian; **Hockey in Canada**, pg.11

[189] Conacher, Brian; **As the Puck Turns**, pg.211

[190] Pelletier, Joe; "Brian Conacher", mapleleaflegends.blogspot.ca, 2007

[191] Conacher, Brian; **Hockey in Canada**, pg. 13

[192] Conacher, Brian; **Hockey in Canada**, pp. 14-15

[193] In a Toronto Daily Star article written in 1937, Lionel was asked about whether he would like his sons to take up sports as a profession. The "Big Train's" response was illuminating about what he expected for his children. He said, my boy can play "all the sports he wants to play. Any sport, any place, any time. But not as a business. No, my boy gets a job where he can live 12 months in every year, not loaf six months and become a slave to a schedule the other six, it's not worth it. "Many Athletes Frown on Sons Taking Up Game", **Toronto Daily Star**, July 23, 1937, pg. 24

[194] Conacher Brian; **Hockey in Canada**, pg. 15

[195] Conacher, Brian; **Hockey in Canada**, pg. 17

[196]Conacher, Brian; **Hockey in Canada**, pg. 17

[197]Conacher, Brian; **As the Puck Turns**, pg. 212

[198] McKee, Ken; "Brian Tops Uncle Charlie", Toronto Star, October 24, 1966, pg. 12

[199] Conacher, Brian; **As the Puck Turns**, pg. 212

[200] Brian Conacher interview on Ontario Morning on CBC Radio, February 13, 2014

[201] Brian Conacher interview on Ontario Morning on CBC Radio, February 13, 2014

[202] Lytle, Andy; "Speaking on Sports". **Toronto Daily Star**, January 9, 1946, pg. 8

[203]Conacher, Brian; **Hockey in Canada**, pp.56-59

[204]Shea, Kevin with Paul Patskou, Roly Harris, & Paul Bruno; **Toronto Maple**

Leafs: Diary of a Dynasty 1957-1967, Firefly, Toronto, 2010, pg. 351

[205] Burnett, Red; "Money, Big Money, is Key to Brian's Hockey Future", **Toronto Daily Star**, September 18, 1965, pg. 40

[206] McKee, Ken; "Brian Tops Uncle Charlie", **Toronto Star**, October 24, 1966, pg. 12

[207] Shea, Kevin, etal; **Toronto Maple Leafs**, pg. 387

[208] Obodiac, Stan; "Brian Conacher: No Hockey Brat He", Hockey Pictorial, December 1967, pg. 37

[209]Shea; **Toronto Maple Leafs**, pg. 416

[210] Obodiac, Stan; "Brian Conacher: No Hockey Brat He", **Hockey Pictorial**, December 1967, pg. 37

[211]Conacher, Brian; **As the Puck Turns**, pp. 214-15

[212]Conacher, Brian; **As the Puck Turns**, pp. 227-228

[213]Traded to Minnesota by Detroit with Danny Lawson for Wayne Connelly, February 15, 1969.

[214]Traded to Toronto by Minnesota with Terry O'Malley and cash for Murray Oliver, May 22, 1970

[215]Traded to Detroit by Toronto for cash, August 20, 1971

[216]SIHR is the Society for International Hockey Research

[217] Conacher, Brian; **As The Puck Turns: A Personal Journey Through the**

World of Hockey, Harper Collins Canada Ltd., Toronto, 2007, pg. 14

[218]Conacher, Brian; **As the Puck Turns**, pg. 15

[219] SIHR data base
[220]Conacher, Brian; **As the Puck Turns**, pg. 78

[221] Conacher; **As the Puck Turns**, pg. 84
[222] Conacher; **As the Puck Turns,** pg. 109
[223] Conacher; As the Puck Turns, pg. 124
[224] Conacher; As the Puck Turns, pg. 129
[225] Conacher; As the Puck Turns, pg. 132
[226] Conacher; As the Puck Turns, pg. 133
[227] Conacher; As the Puck Turns, pg. 142
[228] Conacher; As the Puck Turns' pg. 144
[229] Conacher, AS... pg. 147
[230] Conacher, As...pg. 165
[231] Conacher; As... pg. 258
[232] Conacher; As... pp.258-259
[233] SIHR data base
[234]
[235] Patton, Paul; "Where Are They Now? – Murray Henderson", **Globe and Mail**, September 19, 1987, pg. F4
[236] SIHR data base
[237] SIHR data base
[238] Patton, Paul; "Where Are They Now? – Murray Henderson", **Globe and Mail**, September 19, 1987, pg. F4
[239] Patton, Paul; "Where Are They Now? – Murray Henderson", **Globe and Mail**, September 19, 1987, pg. F4
[240] "Bauer Appointed Bruins' Captain", **Globe and Mail**, October 17, 1946, pg. 18

28322738R20106

Made in the USA
San Bernardino, CA
27 December 2015